HAL LEONARD KEYBOARD STYLE SERIES

INTRO TO JAZZ PIANO

THE COMPLETE GUIDE WITH AUDIO!

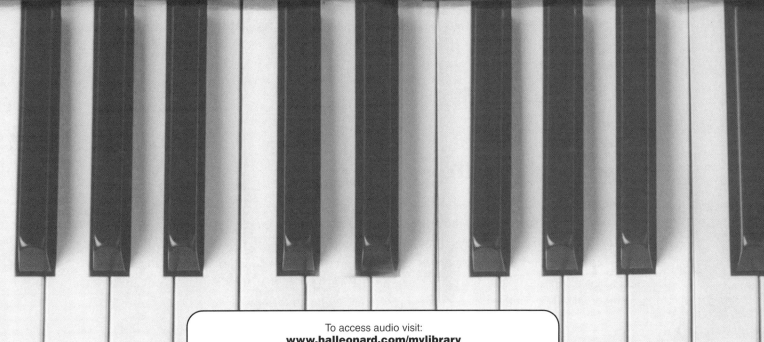

To access audio visit:
www.halleonard.com/mylibrary

Enter Code
6100-2218-2964-2187

BY MARK HARRISON

ISBN 978-1-61780-310-9

HAL•LEONARD®
C O R P O R A T I O N
7777 W. BLUEMOUND RD. P.O. BOX 13819 MILWAUKEE, WI 53213

T0057785

In Australia contact:
Hal Leonard Australia Pty. Ltd.
4 Lentara Court
Cheltenham, Victoria, 3192 Australia
Email: ausadmin@halleonard.com.au

Visit Hal Leonard Online at
www.halleonard.com

INTRODUCTION

Welcome to *Intro to Jazz Piano*. If you want to learn how to play the enduring standards that make up the Great American Songbook, then you've come to the right place! This book gives the beginning-to-intermediate pianist a thorough introduction to the voicings and rhythms needed to play these classic tunes in an authentic way. You'll learn how to accompany another singer or instrumentalist, how to play the melody in a solo piano setting, and how to begin creating improvised solos. You'll also play along with a jazz rhythm section on the audio, while practicing all the examples—a perfect way to prepare for your first (or next) jazz gig.

Five complete songs based on classic jazz standards are included in the "Style File" chapter at the end of the book. These examples include accompaniment, melody treatment, and improvised solo parts. Playing along with the rhythm section on these tunes is a great way to develop your jazz piano chops.

The techniques in this book were pioneered at the world-famous Grove School of Music in Los Angeles, where I had the privilege of teaching for several years. Dick Grove was one of the most important contemporary music educators of the late 20th century, and his concepts have significantly influenced the writing of this *Intro to Jazz Piano* book. Some of my students and customers have graciously said that my music education career has been "keeping the Grove flame alive" into the 21st century, which I take as a compliment of the highest order.

Good luck with playing your Jazz Piano!

–Mark Harrison

About the Audio

On the accompanying audio, you'll find play-along tracks for almost all of the examples in the book. For each track, the rhythm section is on the left channel and the piano is on the right channel. When you want to play along with the band, turn down the right channel to eliminate the recorded piano. When you want to hear the piano part for reference, turn down the left channel to eliminate the rhythm section. This is all designed to give you maximum flexibility when practicing! The rhythm section tracks contain bass and drums, plus a selection of other instruments (jazz organ, guitar, and flute).

About the Author

Mark Harrison is a professional keyboardist, composer/arranger, and music educator/author based in Los Angeles. He has worked with top musicians such as Jay Graydon (Steely Dan), John Molo (Bruce Hornsby band), Jimmy Haslip (Yellowjackets), and numerous others. Mark currently performs with his own contemporary jazz band (the Mark Harrison Quintet) as well as with the Steely Dan tribute band Doctor Wu. His TV music credits include *Saturday Night Live*, *The Montel Williams Show*, *American Justice*, *Celebrity Profiles*, *America's Most Wanted*, *True Hollywood Stories*, the British documentary program *Panorama*, and many others.

Mark taught at the renowned Grove School of Music for six years, instructing hundreds of musicians from all around the world. He currently runs a busy private teaching studio, catering to the needs of professional and aspiring musicians alike. His students include Grammy winners, hit songwriters, members of the Boston Pops and L.A. Philharmonic orchestras, and first-call touring musicians with major acts.

Mark's music instruction books are used by thousands of musicians in over 20 countries, and are recommended by the Berklee College of Music for all their new students. He has also written Master Class articles for *Keyboard* and *How to Jam* magazines, covering a variety of different keyboard styles and topics. For further information on Mark's musical activities, education products, and online lessons, please visit *www.harrisonmusic.com*.

CONTENTS

Chapter 1
JAZZ MUSIC AND JAZZ STANDARDS

Jazz music first emerged in the late 19th century, and then flourished throughout the 20th century and beyond. New Orleans and Dixieland jazz styles first developed in the 1910s and '20s and were noted for both their solo and group improvisation. This was then followed by the Swing era in the 1930s, which emphasized big bands and danceable arrangements. Then in the 1940s many younger musicians broke away from the swing styles to create Bebop or Bop, a less danceable small group style with more advanced harmonies and rhythms. This was in turn followed in the 1950s by the mellower Cool Jazz and the extended improvisation of the Post Bop styles. Then in the 1960s and '70s, the Fusion movement began, combining jazz elements with modern styles such as rock and R&B. All the Contemporary Jazz styles of the late 20th and early 21st centuries are descended from this period. Today, all these jazz styles (modern and traditional) coexist, and are performed and recorded around the world.

Throughout the 20th century, many piano players emerged who were hugely influential in creating the various jazz styles. Jelly Roll Morton was in the forefront of the early New Orleans movement, and immodestly called himself the "inventor of jazz." Art Tatum and Teddy Wilson were giants of the Swing era, followed by Bud Powell and Thelonius Monk, who were trailblazers in the Bebop period. The Post Bop harmonic style of Bill Evans was a major influence on both fusion and mainstream jazz pianists from the 1970s onward, including Chick Corea, Herbie Hancock, Joe Zawinul, and Keith Jarrett.

This book focuses on the piano techniques required to play jazz standards. These are songs that are widely known and performed by successive generations of jazz pianists, and the artists mentioned above are known for their interpretations of these classic tunes. Ironically, many of these songs were not written by jazz composers—most of them are either from Hollywood musicals, Broadway shows, or Tin Pan Alley popular songs. These songs were written from the 1920s to the 1950s and collectively make up the Great American Songbook. They have classic and enduring melodies, offering jazz musicians almost limitless possibilities for melodic, harmonic, and rhythmic interpretation.

Jazz tunes and standards are normally presented in lead sheet form. A lead sheet is a musical chart that shows the melody and chord symbols. When reading a lead sheet, the jazz pianist will then improvise a part based on the chord symbols and melody. This book gives you a foundation for how to do this, using various lead sheet examples based on famous standards.

A fake book is a collection of lead sheets, normally in a particular music style. A good source for jazz standards is *The Real Book, Sixth Edition*, published by Hal Leonard Corporation. Virtually every musician I know in Los Angeles has this book—or a previous edition. Reading and playing these charts is a great way of putting into practice the techniques you'll learn in this *Intro to Jazz Piano* book.

In Chapter 2 we'll get started with some basic voicings and rhythms that you can use in jazz standards. On with the show!

INTRO TO JAZZ PIANO VOICINGS AND COMPING

The II–V–I Progression

The term "II–V–I progression" refers to chords built from the II (second), V (fifth), and I (first) degrees of a key. This progression is the foundation of mainstream jazz harmony, and II–V–I chords are found in many jazz tunes and standards. Jazz styles normally make use of four-part (or larger) chords, as opposed to the triads (three-part chords) commonly found in pop and rock styles.

II–V–I progressions are found in major and minor keys. For now we'll focus on major keys, then later in this book we'll look at these progressions in minor keys. First we'll build four-part chords (sometimes referred to as "seventh chords") from each degree of a C major scale, as follows:

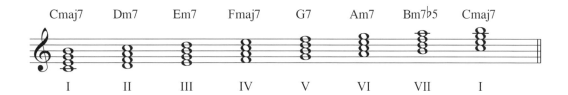

These are known as diatonic four-part chords, as they are all contained within the C major scale. (Diatonic means "belonging to the scale or key.") We'll now review a little theory about these four-part chords:

- The symbols with the "maj7" suffix are **major seventh chords**, created by building major 3rd, perfect 5th and major 7th intervals above the root. This interval pattern occurs in the Cmaj7, and Fmaj7 chords.

- The symbols with the "m7" suffix are **minor seventh chords**, created by building minor 3rd, perfect 5th and minor 7th intervals above the root. This interval pattern occurs in the Dm7, Em7, and Am7 chords.

- The symbol with the "7" suffix is a **dominant seventh chord**, created by building major 3rd, perfect 5th and minor 7th intervals above the root. This interval pattern occurs in the G7 chord.

- The symbol with the "m7♭5" suffix is a **minor seventh with flatted 5th chord**, created by building minor 3rd, diminished 5th, and minor 7th intervals above the root (equivalent to flatting the 5th of a minor seventh chord by half-step). This interval pattern occurs in the Bm7♭5 chord.

Note that Roman numerals are shown below each chord, indicating the function of each chord within the key. So in the key of C, the Dm7 is a II (or "two chord"), the G7 is a V (or "five chord"), and the C major seventh chord is a I (or "one chord"). Next we will combine these II, V, and I chords as follows:

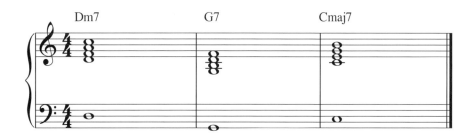

TRACK 1

We now have a root note in the bass clef for each chord (D, G, and C respectively), below the four-part chords in the treble clef. In the right hand we are playing each chord exactly as it is spelled, i.e., playing the root-3rd-5th-7th of each chord, from bottom to top. While this may sometimes be OK, it is more common for jazz pianists to **voice** these chords for stylistic effect. A **voicing** is a specific interpretation of a chord symbol by the pianist. This may involve adding extensions or alterations to the basic chord symbol, subtracting notes from the basic chord symbol, redistributing the notes between the hands, and so on.

Seven-Three Chord Voicings

The first and most fundamental jazz piano voicing we will work on is the "seven-three" voicing. This involves playing just the seventh and third of each chord in the right hand, over the root of the chord in the left hand. This also gives us very good "voice leading" (moving by common tones or small intervals) between successive chords in the II–V–I progression, as in the following example:

TRACK 2

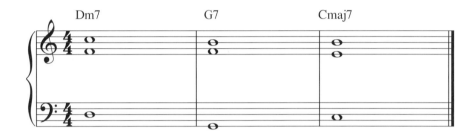

When we isolate the sevenths and thirds of the chords in this way, each voicing is very "definitive," as these chord tones precisely define each chord quality, as follows:

- On the Dm7 chord, the 3rd (F) is a minor 3rd interval above the root (D), and the 7th (C) is a minor 7th interval above the root (D). This combination of minor 3rd and minor 7th intervals above the root explicitly defines a minor 7th chord quality.

- On the G7 chord, the 3rd (B) is a major 3rd interval above the root (G), and the 7th (F) is a minor 7th interval above the root (G). This combination of major 3rd and minor 7th intervals above the root explicitly defines a dominant 7th chord quality. The 3rd is now voiced above the 7th on this chord, in order to voice lead smoothly from the previous chord.

- On the Cmaj7 chord, the 3rd (E) is a major 3rd interval above the root (C), and the 7th (B) is a major 7th interval above the root (C). This combination of major 3rd and major 7th intervals above the root explicitly defines a major 7th chord quality.

In order to build seven-three voicings over II–V–I progressions, you'll need to know the 3rds and 7ths of all the major 7th, minor 7th, and dominant 7th chords. The exercises in this book will help you learn these as needed. Note that the least definitive of the chord tones (the 5th) is omitted from these voicings. All of these chords include perfect 5ths, and so this does not help us define each chord quality. The 5th of a chord is never definitive unless it is altered. More about this later on.

Let's look at the voice leading between these chords in more detail:

- The 7th of the Dm7 chord (C) moves by half-step to the 3rd of the G7 chord (B).
- The 3rd of the Dm7 chord (F) becomes the 7th of the G7 chord.
- The 3rd of the G7 chord (B) becomes the 7th of the Cmaj7 chord.
- The 7th of the G7 chord (F) moves by half-step to the 3rd of the Cmaj7 chord (E).

This very "leading" sound between the definitive tones across the II–V–I progression is a very important harmonic characteristic of mainstream jazz styles.

In the next example, we have flipped the 7-3 voices, so that the 3rd (F) is now on top of the first Dm7 chord, as follows:

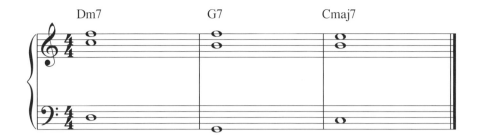

TRACK 3

Again note that we are voice leading smoothly from left to right, now with the bottom treble clef line in Track 2 (F–F–E) moved up to the top voice. It's important to be able to voice lead across the II–V–I progression in both of these ways (i.e., starting with either the 7th or 3rd on top of the first chord), as we will soon see!

Jazz Swing Comping Rhythms (Swing Eighths)

Now we'll start to rhythmically rephrase these II–V–I progressions for a jazz swing feel. Most mainstream jazz uses a "swing eighths" rhythmic subdivision. This means that, instead of eighth notes dividing the beat exactly in half, the beat is instead divided in a two-thirds/one-third ratio. This contrasts with a "straight eighths" rhythmic subdivision, in which the eighth notes divide the beat exactly in half.

Swing eighths music is normally written the same way as straight eighths, but with either a written description or symbol above the music indicating that the eighth notes are to be swung:

$$\textbf{Swing eighths} \text{ or } (\; \sqcap = \overset{\ulcorner 3 \urcorner}{\flat \; \flat} \;)$$

We can hear this rhythmic feel in the following jazz swing interpretation of the II–V–I voicings used in Track 2:

TRACK 4

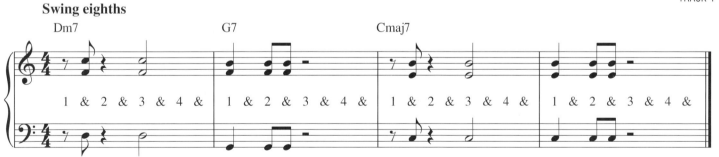

As you listen to Track 4, you'll hear that the rhythm section is on the left channel, and the piano part shown above is on the right channel. Notice that the rhythmic counting (1 & 2 & 3 & 4 &) is shown below the treble clef, for each measure. This is the way we normally count eighth-note rhythms, with the 1, 2, 3, and 4 falling on the **downbeats**, and the "&s" in between falling on the **upbeats**. Don't forget that with this swing-eighths example, all the "&s" occur two-thirds of the way through each beat, which gives the rhythm a more "loping" or "shuffle" type of feel. Try counting along with the audio track as needed, to get comfortable with this rhythmic idea.

Track 4 is our first example of **jazz swing** rhythmic "comping" (accompaniment). We would call this a "two-measure phrase," because the rhythm repeats every two measures. One-, two-, and four-measure rhythmic phrases are commonly used in jazz and contemporary styles.

Note that each measure contains some combination of rhythmic events landing on downbeats (on the beat, i.e., 1, 2, 3, or 4) and upbeats (on the "&s" in between, i.e., the "& of 1," "& of 2," "& of 3," or "& of 4"). When a rhythmic event landing on an upbeat is followed by a rest on the following downbeat, or is sustained through the following downbeat, this is called an **anticipation**. With these points in mind, let's analyze the rhythms in Track 4 as follows:

Measure 1   The first Dm7 voicing lands on the "& of 1" and is followed by a rest on beat 2. This is therefore an anticipation of beat 2. The next Dm7 voicing lands on beat 3.

Measure 2   The G7 voicings land on beats 1, 2, and the "& of 2." The last voicing is followed by a rest on beat 3. This is therefore an anticipation of beat 3.

Measures 3–4   Same rhythm as for measures 1–2.

These rhythmic anticipations are an important component of the jazz swing "rhythmic feel." Time for another jazz swing comping example, this time using the II–V–I voicings from Track 3:

Swing eighths

TRACK 5

Again note the rhyhmic counting shown below the treble clef. We can analyze this two-measure rhythmic phrase as follows:

Measure 1   The Dm7 voicings land on beats 1, 3, and the "& of 3." The last voicing is followed by a rest on beat 4. This is therefore an anticipation of beat 4.

Measure 2   The G7 voicings land on beat 1 and the "& of 2." The last voicing is tied over to beat 3. This is therefore an anticipation of beat 3.

Measures 3–4   Same rhythm as for measures 1–2.

We will play more jazz swing rhythmic comping variations as we progress through this book. Stay tuned!

Bossa Nova Comping Rhythms (Straight Eighths)

Next we'll rhythmically rephrase these II–V–I progressions for a bossa nova feel. Most Latin styles (including bossa nova) use a "straight eighths" rhythmic subdivision, i.e., the eighth notes divide the beat exactly in half. Here's our first **bossa nova** comping pattern, using the II–V–I voicings from Track 2:

TRACK 6

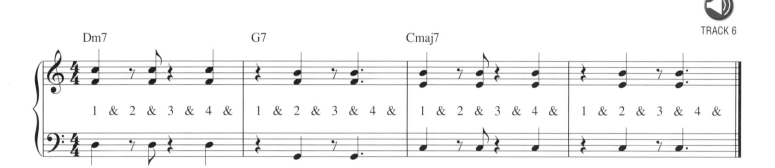

Listen to Track 6 and you'll hear the difference between the "straight eighths" bossa nova style and the "swing eighths" feel of the previous jazz swing examples. Again note that each measure contains voicings that land on downbeats and upbeats, as analyzed below:

Measure 1   The Dm7 voicings land on beat 1, the "& of 2," and beat 4. The middle voicing is followed by a rest on beat 3 and is therefore an anticipation of beat 3.

Measure 2   The G7 voicings land on beat 2 and the "& of 3." The last voicing is sustained through beat 4. This is therefore an anticipation of beat 4.

Measures 3–4   Same rhythm as for measures 1–2.

This is considered the standard or "default" bossa nova rhythm, but there are numerous variations possible, including the next bossa nova comping example based on the II–V–I voicings heard in Track 3:

TRACK 7

Again note the rhythmic counting shown below the treble clef. We can analyze this two-measure rhythmic phrase as follows:

Measure 1   The Dm7 voicings land on beats 1, 2, and the "& of 3," which anticipates beat 4. The G7 voicing then lands on the "& of 4," which is an anticipation of the following beat 1.

Measure 2   The remaining G7 voicings land on the "& of 2" and the "& of 3," anticipating beats 3 and 4 respectively.

Measures 3–4   Same rhythm as for measures 1–2.

Later on, we'll look at more bossa nova rhythmic comping variations and apply them to chord progressions used in some famous bossa nova songs.

Before we continue, we need to take care of one more music theory topic. Some of the exercises in this book move through all the keys in either a Circle of 5ths or Circle of 4ths sequence, so we need to make sure we understand what is meant by these terms.

Circle of 5ths and Circle of 4ths Review

The Circle of 5ths (and Circle of 4ths) is often shown as a diagram, like this:

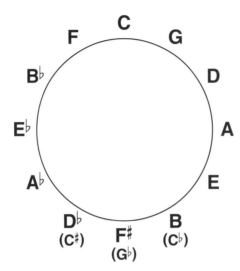

Each of the entries around the circle can represent a major key. The terms Circle of 5ths and Circle of 4ths refer to the different movement directions (i.e., clockwise or counter-clockwise) around the circle. In my books and classes, I define these directions on a harmonic basis. For example, if we move from the key of C to the key of G, one clockwise movement from the top of the circle, we can define this as a four-to-one (IV–I) movement with respect to the key of G where we have landed. This direction can then be termed Circle of 4ths. Similarly, if we move from the key of C to the key of F, one counter-clockwise movement from the top of the circle, we can define this as a five-to-one (V-I) movement with respect to the key of F where we have landed. This direction can then be termed Circle of 5ths.

So within this book, Circle of 5ths refers to a sequence of keys (beginning on C) as follows:
C–F–B♭–E♭–A♭–D♭–G♭–B–E–A–D–G (Think "C is the V of F, F is the V of B♭," and so on.)

Also within this book, Circle of 4ths refers to a sequence of keys (beginning on C) as follows:
C–G–D–A–E–B–G♭–D♭–A♭–E♭–B♭–F (Think "C is the IV of G, G is the IV of D," and so on.)
You should be aware that there are different interpretations of what is meant by Circle of 5ths and Circle of 4ths across a wide range of textbooks and methods. For further information about this topic, please check out my other Hal Leonard publications: *All About Music Theory* and *Contemporary Music Theory, Level One*.

Major 7th, Minor 7th, and Dominant 7th Chords in All Keys

As you can see, it will be important to get these seven-three voicings under your fingers in all keys. The first stage in this process is to learn and play these voicings on each type of chord found in the II–V–I progression (minor 7th, dominant 7th, and major 7th) individually. This will then provide a good foundation when using the voicings within a progression, such as II–V–I.

Your ability to do this will depend on how quickly you can recall the type of 3rd and 7th interval present in each of these chords, as discussed in the text following Track 2. Here's a quick summary of these intervals:

The **major 7th chord** contains major 3rd and major 7th intervals up from the root. For example:

- The 3rd of a Cmaj7 chord is E. (C up to E is a major 3rd interval.)
- The 7th of a Cmaj7 chord is B. (C up to B is a major 7th interval.)

The **minor 7th chord** contains minor 3rd and minor 7th intervals up from the root. For example:

- The 3rd of a Dm7 chord is F. (D up to F is a minor 3rd interval.)
- The 7th of a Dm7 chord is C. (D up to C is a minor 7th interval.)

The **dominant 7th chord** contains major 3rd and minor 7th intervals up from the root. For example:

- The 3rd of a G7 chord is B. (G up to B is a major 3rd interval.)
- The 7th of a G7 chord is F. (G up to F is a minor 7th interval.)

Some students find it helpful to make flashcards for themselves, with a card for each major 7th, minor 7th, and dominant 7th chord. (You can write the chord symbol on the front, and the seven-three voicing on the back.) For further information about deriving intervals and spelling chords, please refer to my *Contemporary Music Theory, Level One* book, published by Hal Leonard Corporation.

For variety, the exercises in this section contain backing tracks in either a jazz swing or bossa nova feel. However, for now we are just playing the voicings as whole notes lasting four beats each. First up, we have all the major 7th chords in a Circle of 5ths sequence, starting with the Cmaj7 chord. This exercise requires you to place the 7th on top of each seven-three voicing:

(Backing track: Jazz Swing)

TRACK 8

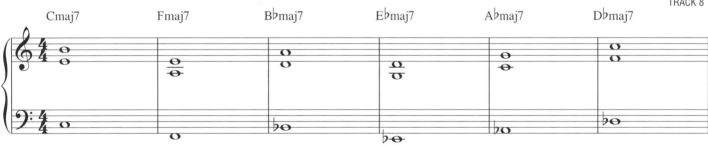

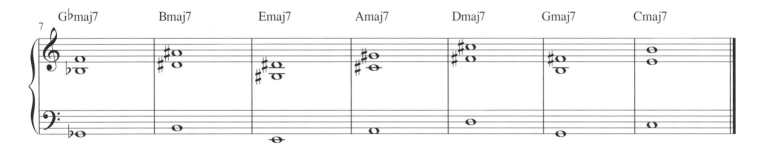

Note that larger interval skips are required between the voicings, as we are not "voice leading" between the changes. This prompts you to learn these voicings individually, which will then help in combining them together in various progressions.

Next we have the same major 7th chords, this time with the 3rd on top of each:

(Backing track: Bossa Nova)

TRACK 9

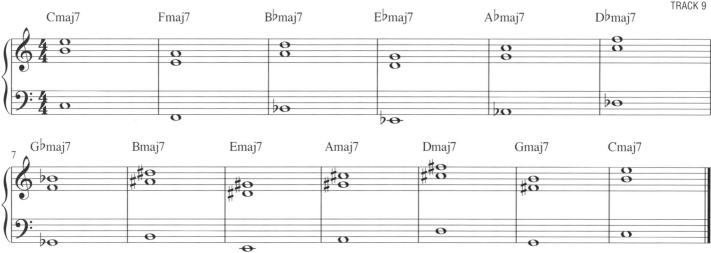

Next we have all the minor 7th chords in a Circle of 5ths sequence, starting with the Cm7 chord. Again we start by placing the 7th on top of each seven-three voicing:

(Backing track: Jazz Swing)

TRACK 10

Next we have the same minor 7th chords, this time with the 3rd on top of each:

(Backing track: Bossa Nova)

TRACK 11

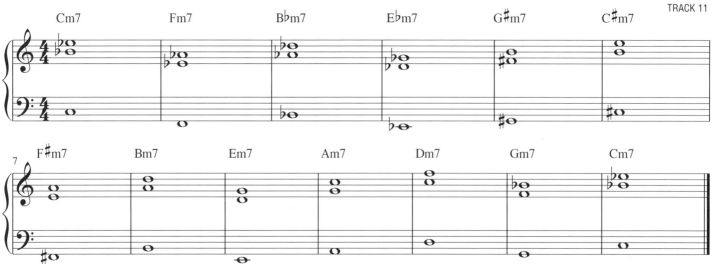

Finally in this section we have all the dominant 7th chords in a Circle of 5ths sequence, starting with the C7 chord. Again we start by placing the 7th on top of each seven-three voicing:

(Backing track: Jazz Swing)

TRACK 12

Next we have the same dominant 7th chords, this time with the 3rd on top of each:

(Backing track: Bossa Nova)

TRACK 13

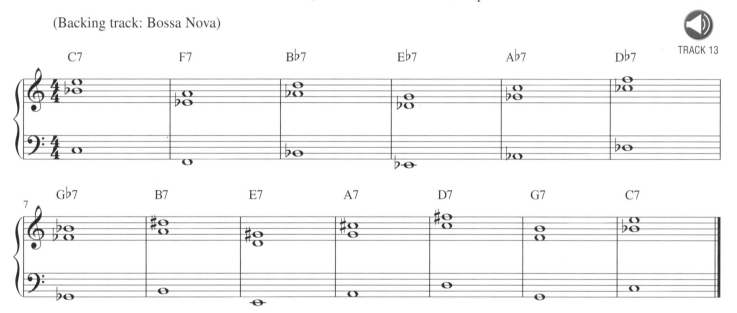

Once you are comfortable with all of the major 7th, minor 7th, and dominant 7th voicings in Tracks 8–13, you should aim to play them from memory (i.e., without reading the notes). You can do this by looking at the Circle of 5ths diagram back on page 10 to prompt you for the sequence of chords required.

II–V–I Progressions in All Keys (Seven-Three Voicings)

Next we'll apply all of the previous major 7th, minor 7th, and dominant 7th voicings when playing II–V–I progressions in all keys. Here we'll be voice leading closely through the changes, as we first saw in Tracks 2 and 3. Our first example in this section starts with the 7th on top of the Dm7 chord in the key of C (as in Track 2), and then voice leads through all the remaining keys in a Circle of 5ths sequence as follows:

(Backing track: Jazz Swing)

TRACK 14

Note that the keys in this example are moving in a Circle of 5ths sequence: We start with II–V–I in C, followed by II–V–I in F, followed by II–V–I in B♭, and so on. To voice lead starting with the 7th on top of the first Dm7 chord, we had the "7-3-7" line on top for the key of C (i.e., 7th of the Dm7, 3rd of the G7, and 7th of the Cmaj7) as first seen in Track 2. Then to voice lead closely into the II–V–I progression in F, the seven-three lines were flipped over, so that we had the "3-7-3" line on top for the key of F (i.e., 3rd of the Gm7, 7th of the C7, and 3rd of the Fmaj7). This alternation of the seven-three lines then continued for the remaining keys.

Therefore, had we started with the 3rd on top of the first Dm7 chord (as in Track 3), all the subsequent seven-three lines would have been flipped over to ensure smooth voice leading between the keys, as follows:

(Backing track: Bossa Nova)

Once you are comfortable with these II–V–I exercises, you should aim to play them from memory (i.e., without reading the notes). Again, you can do this by looking at the Circle of 5ths diagram back on page 10, to prompt you for the sequence of keys required.

Now it's time to apply comping rhythms to these II–V–I progressions through all keys in a Circle of 5ths sequence, beginning with an example in a jazz swing style. You'll remember from Tracks 4 and 5 that the jazz swing style is based on a swing eighths rhythmic subdivision. This example starts with the 7th on top of the first Dm7 chord, and follows the seven-three voice leading that we saw in Track 14. Don't forget to play the upbeats two-thirds of the way through the beat (see comments following Track 4), as needed for the jazz swing feel:

TRACK 16

Swing eighths

This example uses the two-measure jazz swing rhythmic phrase from Track 4, repeated throughout all the keys.

Our next example is in a **bossa nova** style. You'll remember from Tracks 6 and 7 that the bossa nova style is based on a straight-eighths rhythmic subdivision. This example starts with the 3rd on top of the first Dm7 chord, and follows the seven-three voice leading that we saw in Track 15, through all the keys in a Circle of 5ths sequence. Don't forget to play the upbeats exactly halfway through the beat, as needed for the bossa nova feel:

TRACK 17

This example uses the two-measure bossa nova rhythmic phrase from Track 7, repeated throughout all the keys.

II–V–I Progressions in All Keys (Seven-Three Voicings with Doubling)

Next we'll add some important variations to strengthen the seven-three voicing using "doubling," which means repeating one or more of the seven-three voices in different octaves. We will do this as follows:

Right hand   Double the top note one octave lower, with the thumb. If the 7th is on top, then we'll add another 7th one octave lower, resulting in 7th-3rd-7th from top to bottom. If the 3rd is on top, then we'll add another 3rd one octave lower, resulting in 3rd-7th-3rd from top to bottom.

Left hand   Add the 7th above the root in the left hand, range permitting. This will sound muddy if played too low. You can get away with this down to the E♭ at the bottom of the bass clef for minor 7th intervals (needed for minor 7th and dominant 7th chords) and down to the F at the bottom of the bass clef for major 7th intervals (needed for major 7th chords).

If the left hand is too low to play the root-7th interval, and/or the right hand is too close to the left hand, then adding the 5th above the root is another option. The general rule of thumb is: always add the root-7th in the left hand if the range permits. This is a stylistic jazz sound. By contrast, the root-5th is never necessary in the left hand, but used sparingly can be useful as a textural thickening of the voicing. So, don't default to root-5th if you don't have room for root-7th in the left hand: just playing the root, as we were doing before, will work fine. (Root-5th in the left hand is very common in pop and rock styles, but is not a definitive or necessary jazz sound.) We will see these various guidelines at work in the following examples.

On to our first seven-three voicing example using doubling. This is based on the voice leading and top notes through all the keys in a Circle of 5ths sequence that we saw in Track 14, transposed up an octave. The right hand is playing either 7th-3rd-7th or 3rd-7th-3rd on each chord, and the left hand is playing root-7th (and some root-5th) intervals:

(Backing track: Jazz Swing)

TRACK 18

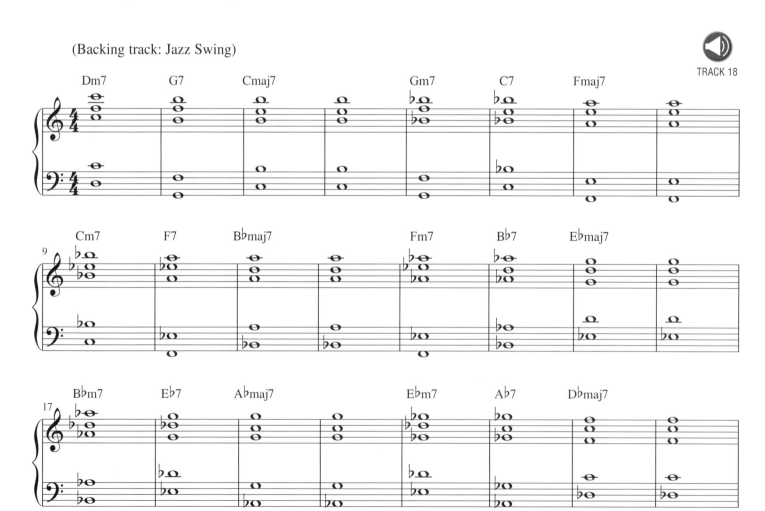

20

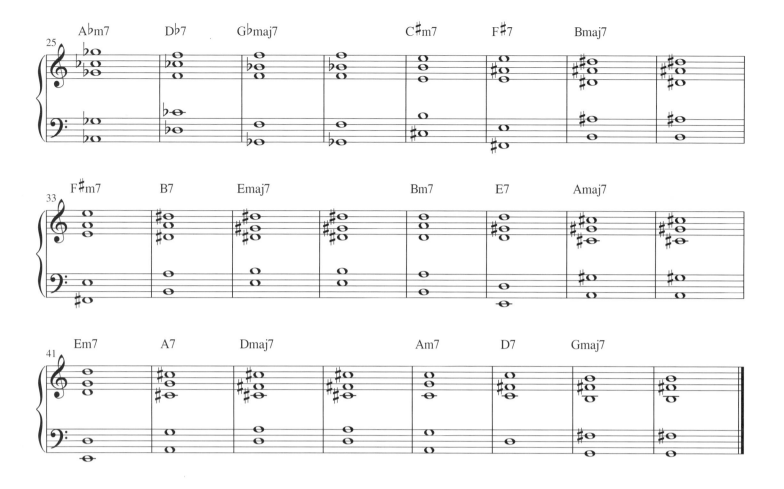

Note that in this example we had room to play root-7th intervals in the left hand, except in the following situations:

Measures 35–36	The low root-7th (E up to D♯) on the Emaj7 chord would have been below our "range limit" of F for the left hand major 7th intervals, so we chose the root-5th option. The root-5th could have been played higher, as here, or an octave lower. For better voicing balance, I have a mild preference for the higher position.
Measures 43–44:	On the Dmaj7 chord, similar situation to the Emaj7 chord above.
Measure 46	The low root-7th (D up to C) on the D7 chord would have been below our "range limit" of E♭ for the left hand minor 7th intervals, so in this case we chose simply to play the root.

Now we'll get back into a jazz swing rhythmic style, using these seven-three voicings with doubling through all the keys, again in a Circle of 5ths sequence. This example uses the two-measure jazz swing rhythmic phrase from Track 5, repeated throughout all the keys:

TRACK 19

Swing eighths

Comping through "Autumn Leaves" (Jazz Swing)

Now we'll put these voicings and rhythms to work as we "comp through the changes" to some well-known songs. For now, when we apply a basic seven-three voicing approach to a song, we will essentially reduce all chord symbols to four-part chords, which will almost always be either the major 7th, minor 7th, or dominant 7th chords used so far. In other words, if we see a major 9th chord symbol, we will treat it as a major 7th. If we see a dominant 13th chord symbol, we will treat it as a dominant 7th, and so on. This still gives us the basic "definitive" tones of the chord, and will be sufficient in many situations. Later on we will see how to add other chord tones/extensions to the basic seven-three voicing.

We'll start with the chord progression commonly used for "Autumn Leaves," one of the most-performed jazz standards of all time. First we have the seven-three voicings, with doubling of the 3rds and/or 7ths as shown in the previous section, using whole-note rhythms:

(Backing track: Jazz Swing)

TRACK 20

(If you are familiar with this song, you may know that the F♯m7 and B7 chord symbols in this example are often shown on fake book charts as F♯m7⁻5 and B7⁻9 respectively. These chord symbols have been simplified in this example to reflect the seven-three voicing approach being used. Later in this book we will see how to add the ⁻5 and ⁻9 to these chords. In a real-world situation, you could still play just the seven-three voicing on these chords if desired).

24

Note that we are voice leading between chords (i.e., moving by close intervals), with some larger intervals being used occasionally. Next up is a jazz swing rhythmic treatment using these voicings and voice leading, suitable for comping through the changes on this song:

The rhythmic comping in this example consists of four-measure phrases, each of which in turn contains two two-measure phrases. Measures 1–2 use the swing rhythm first seen in Track 4, and measures 3–4 use the swing rhythm first seen in Track 5. These measures combine to create a four-measure phrase, which is then repeated during measures 5–8, and so on.

This example, like the chord progressions for many standard tunes, contains several II–V–I progressions. For much more information on how II–V–I progressions work in major and minor keys, please refer to my *Contemporary Music Theory, Level Two* book, published by Hal Leonard Corporation.

Comping through "Blue Bossa" (Bossa Nova)

Next up is the chord progression commonly used for "Blue Bossa," a well-known bossa nova standard. Again we first have the seven-three voicings with doubling, using whole-note rhythms:

(Backing track: Bossa nova)

TRACK 22

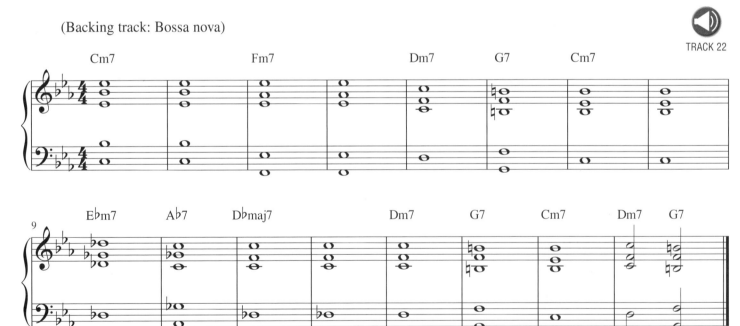

(If you are familiar with this song, you may know that the Dm7 and G7 chord symbols in this example are often shown on fake book charts as Dm7⁻5 and G7⁻9 respectively. These chord symbols have been simplified in this example to reflect the seven-three voicing approach being used. Later in this book we will see how to add the ⁻5 and ⁻9 to these chords. In a real-world situation, you could still play just the seven-three voicing on these chords if desired).

Our final example in this chapter is a bossa nova rhythmic treatment using these voicings and voice leading, suitable for comping through the changes on this song:

Note that the first half of this example (measures 1–8) uses the rhythm pattern from Track 6, and the second half (measures 9–16) uses the rhythm pattern from Track 7. The busier rhythm in the second half of this example helps to build the energy of the arrangement.

Chapter 3

MORE JAZZ PIANO VOICINGS AND PATTERNS

Left-Hand Jazz Swing Pattern "In 2," applied to "Autumn Leaves"

Next we'll explore some different left-hand patterns used for jazz comping. So far our voicings have been "concerted," that is to say the left and right hands have been playing the same rhythms. As an alternative to this, the left-hand part can play more of a "bass line" role. This is normally done either "in 2" (based on two half-notes per measure, landing on beats 1 and 3) or "in 4" (based on four quarter-notes per measure, landing on beats 1, 2, 3, and 4).

Our first example is based on the seven-three voicings with doubling, used for the "Autumn Leaves" chord progression in Track 20. Here we've taken measures 1–16 of these changes and applied a left hand jazz swing pattern "in 2," as follows:

TRACK 24

Note that the seven-three voicings with doubling in the right hand are the same as used for measures 1–16 of Track 20. The left hand is now playing the root and 5th of each chord, on beats 1 and 3 of each measure respectively. For example, in the first measure in the bass clef we have an A (the root of the Am7 chord) landing on beat 1, and an E (the 5th of the Am7 chord) landing on beat 3. Then in the second measure we have a D (the root of the D7 chord) landing on beat 1, and an A (the 5th of the D7 chord) landing on beat 3, and so on.

In the left hand we also have some eighth-note pickups leading into beat 3. These added notes repeat the root of the chord on the "& of 2," before playing the 5th of the chord on beat 3. This helps add forward motion to the jazz swing feel. Also, in measures 9–14 another eighth-note pickup is added, landing on the "& of 4" and leading into beat 1 of the following measure. This extra note often leads into the next chord root by a half-step interval. For example, in measure 9 after playing the 5th of the Am7 chord (E) on beat 3 in the left hand, we then play E♭ on the "& of 4," leading into the following chord root (D) by half step.

Note also that we are now showing the F♯m7♭5 chord symbol for measures 5 and 13, compared to the more basic F♯m7 symbol used in Track 20. The F♯m7♭5 is the correct chord symbol for this song, although we can get away with playing just the seven-three voices as previously noted. However, if we are going to play the 5th on this chord, which we are now adding in the left hand on beat 3, then we need to ensure that the 5th is flatted. The C natural landing on beat 3 of measures 5 and 13 is the ♭5th of the F♯m7♭5 chord.

Next we'll add some jazz swing rhythms to the right-hand part, while keeping the left-hand pattern "in 2" from the previous example:

TRACK 25

29

Depending on your experience level, you may find some difficulty in rhythmically coordinating the hands for this example. You can practice hands separately as needed, before playing hands together. The key here is to get the left-hand pattern on autopilot as much as possible, so you can then focus on the rhythmic variations and anticipations in the right-hand part.

Left-Hand Bossa Nova Pattern "In 2," applied to "Blue Bossa"

Next we'll look at a straight-eighths version of this type of left hand pattern "in 2," suitable for a bossa nova comping groove. This example is based on the seven-three voicings with doubling, used for the "Blue Bossa" chord progression in Track 22:

TRACK 26

The left hand is again playing the root and 5th of each chord, on beats 1 and 3 of each measure respectively. For example, in measures 1–2 in the bass clef we have a C (the root of the Cm7 chord) landing on beat 1, and a G (the 5th of the Cm7 chord) landing on beat 3. Then in measures 3–4 we have an F (the root of the Fm7 chord) landing on beat 1, and a C (the 5th of the Fm7 chord) landing on beat 3, and so on. This is all very similar to the jazz swing left-hand pattern "in 2" we used on the "Autumn Leaves" progression, except that we are now using a straight-eighths, rather than swing-eighths, rhythmic subdivision.

We are also playing eighth-note pickups in the left hand: the root of each chord landing on the "& of 2" in each measure (leading into the 5th of each chord on beat 3), and either a chord tone or half step connecting tone landing on the "& of 4" in measures 9–15 (leading into the root of the next chord on beat 1).

Note also that we are now showing the Dm7♭5 chord symbol for measures 5, 13, and 16, compared to the more basic Dm7 symbol used in Track 22. The Dm7♭5 is the correct chord symbol for this song, although we can get away with playing just the seven-three voices as previously noted. However, if we are going to play the 5th on this chord, which we are now adding in the left hand on beat 3, then we need to ensure that the 5th is flatted. The A♭ landing on beat 3 of measures 5 and 13, and on the "& of 2" of measure 16, is the ♭5th of the Dm7♭5 chord.

Next we'll add some bossa nova rhythms to the right-hand part, while keeping the left hand pattern "in 2" from the previous example:

Again if you find some difficulty in rhythmically coordinating the hands for this example, you can practice hands separately as needed, before playing hands together. As with the preceding jazz swing example "in 2," the key here is to get the left-hand pattern on autopilot as much as possible.

Seven-Three Extended Chord Voicings

Now it's time to further develop our seven-three chord voicings by adding some extra chord tones in the right hand when accompanying. We may do this in response to a particular chord symbol, or if we are **upgrading** (adding unaltered upper extensions such as the 9th or 13th) or **altering** a basic chord symbol in some way.

These added chord tones fall into two general categories:

Chord tones/extensions	These are the 5th, 9th, and 13th of the chord. Unaltered 5ths and 9ths are normally safe to add to major 7th, minor 7th, and dominant 7th chords in most contexts (unless the chord symbol indicates that one or more of these is altered, i.e., sharped or flatted). Unaltered 13ths are also often added to dominant 7th chords (unless the chord symbol indicates that the 13th is altered, i.e., flatted).
Alterations	These are the ♭5th and ♯5th, and (on dominant chords only) the ♭9th and ♯9th. These are added either in response to an altered chord symbol (e.g., Dm7♭5), or are added by the jazz musician to alter the chord depending on style and context. *(Note that the ⁻5th is equivalent to the ♯11 and the ♯5th is equivalent to the ⁻13 on the chord.)*

Seven-three voicings can be extended in different ways, depending on whether the 3rd or 7th of the voicing is on top. The most common combinations are as follows:

If the **3rd is on top** of the seven-three voicing, then we can add another chord tone above the 3rd in the right hand, depending on the chord symbol and type:

- We can add the 5th on major 7th, minor 7th, or dominant 7th chords.
- We can add the ♭5th on minor 7th(♭5) chords, or to alter minor 7th chords.
- We can add the ♯5th (♭13th) on dominant 7th(♯5) or (♭13) chords, or to alter dominant 7th chords.
- We can add the 13th on dominant 13th chords, or to upgrade dominant 7th or 9th chords.

If the **7th is on top** of the seven-three voicing, then we can add another chord tone above the 7th in the right hand, depending on the chord symbol and type:

- We can add the 9th on major 9th, minor 9th, or dominant 9th chords, or to upgrade major 7th, minor 7th, or dominant 7th chords respectively.
- We can add the ♭9th or ♯9th on dominant 7th(♭9) or (♯9) chords respectively, or to alter dominant 7th chords.

Next we'll see some of these rules at work on II–V–I progressions in the keys of C major and C minor. The right hand is now playing three-note voicings (seven-three plus one extra note on top) on each chord. Here's the II–V–I progression in C major:

TRACK 28

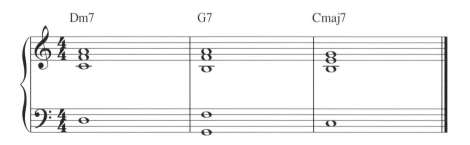

We can analyze these seven-three extended voicings as follows:

Measure 1   The 5th of the Dm7 chord (A) has been added on top of the 3rd (F).

Measure 2   The 9th of the G7 chord (A) has been added on top of the 7th (F), technically upgrading this chord to a G9. We have also added a root-7th interval in the left hand.

Measure 3   The 5th of the Cmaj7 chord (G) has been added on top of the 3rd (E).

Without these added top notes in the right hand, this example would been like the II–V–I voicings shown in Track 3 (seven-three voicings starting with the 3rd on top), but transposed down by one octave. Note that the seven-three extended voicings sound fuller and denser than the basic seven-three voicings. Next up is the corresponding II–V–I progression in C minor:

TRACK 29

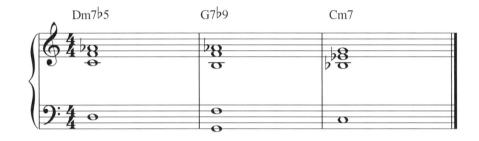

We can analyze these seven-three extended voicings as follows:

Measure 1   The ♭5th of the Dm7♭5 chord (A♭) has been added on top of the 3rd (F).

Measure 2   The ♭9th of the G7♭9 chord (A♭) has been added on top of the 7th (F). Again we have added a root-7th interval in the left hand.

Measure 3   The 5th of the Cm7 chord (G) has been added on top of the 3rd (E♭).

In minor keys, we often see the minor 7th(♭5) functioning as a II chord, and the dominant 7th(♭9) functioning as a V chord, respectively. The I chord will either be a minor 7th chord, as shown here, or a minor major 7th or minor 6th chord.

For much more information on II–V–I progressions in major and minor keys, please refer to my *Contemporary Music Theory, Level Two* book, published by Hal Leonard Corporation.

For much more information on upper extensions and alterations of all commonly used chords, please refer to my *Contemporary Music Theory, Level Three* book, published by Hal Leonard Corporation.

Next we will use these seven-three extended voicings on the chord progression for "Autumn Leaves." This example uses the same right-hand rhythms and left-hand pattern "in 2" that we saw in Track 25, now with extended three-note right-hand voicings:

TRACK 30

We can analyze the seven-three extended voicings in this example as follows:

Measure 1   The 5th of the Am7 chord (E) has been added on top of the 3rd (C).

Measure 2   The 9th of the D7 chord (E) has been added on top of the 7th (C), upgrading this chord to a D9.

Measure 3   The 5th of the Gmaj7 chord (D) has been added on top of the 3rd (B).

Measure 4   The 9th of the Cmaj7 chord (D) has been added on top of the 7th (B), upgrading this chord to a Cmaj9.

Measure 5   The ♭5th of the F♯m7b5 chord (C) has been added on top of the 3rd (A).

Measure 6   The ♭9th of the B7 chord (C) has been added on top of the 7th (A), altering this chord to a B7♭9.

Measures 7–8   The 5th of the Em7 chord (B) has been added on top of the 3rd (G).

Measures 9–16   Same as for measures 1–8.

Now let's see some of these seven-three extended voicings at work on the chord progression for "Blue Bossa." This example uses the same right-hand rhythms and left-hand pattern "in 2" that we saw in Track 27, now with extended three-note right-hand voicings:

TRACK 31

We can analyze the seven-three extended voicings in this example as follows:

Measures 1–2, 7–8, 15	The 5th of the Cm7 chord (G) has been added on top of the 3rd (E♭).
Measures 3–4	The 9th of the Fm7 chord (G) has been added on top of the 7th (E♭), upgrading this chord to an Fm9.
Measures 5, 13, 16	The ♭5th of the Dm7♭5 chord (A♭) has been added on top of the 3rd (F).
Measures 6, 14, 16	The ♭9th of the G7 chord (A♭) has been added on top of the 7th (F), altering this chord to a G7♭9.
Measure 9	The 5th of the E♭m7 chord (B♭) has been added on top of the 3rd (G♭).
Measure 10	The 9th of the A♭7 chord (B♭) has been added on top of the 7th (G♭), upgrading this chord to an A♭9.
Measures 11–12	The 5th of the D♭maj7 chord (A♭) has been added on top of the 3rd (F).

Left-Hand Jazz Swing Pattern "In 4," applied to "All the Things You Are"

As mentioned in the introduction to this chapter, a left-hand bass line "in 4" is based on four quarter notes per measure (landing on beats 1, 2, 3, and 4). This is also referred to as a "walking" bass part in jazz circles.

Our first example of a left hand pattern "in 4" uses the chord progression for "All the Things You Are," another famous jazz standard. The right hand is playing seven-three voicings with doubling, as follows:

TRACK 32

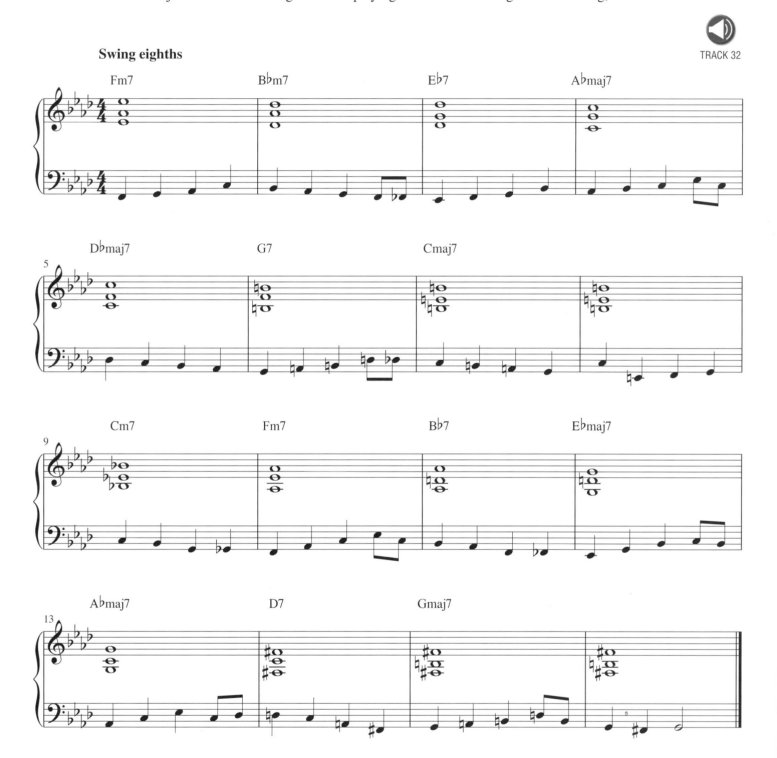

In addition to landing on all the downbeats in each measure, the left-hand part is also playing an extra eighth note on the "& of 4" in some measures. This creates forward motion into beat 1 of the following measure. Walking bass lines are typically constructed from some combination of chord tones/arpeggios, scale tones, and half-step connecting lines. Here are some general guidelines for creating this type of left hand-bass pattern:

- The root of the chord is almost always played on beat 1 of each measure, except when a chord change is continuing into a second measure. In this case, other basic chord tones (i.e., 3rd, 5th, or 7th) can be used on beat 1 of the second measure.

- Once you know the register (high or low) in which you want to play the root of the next chord, you can then design an ascending or descending line during the preceding measure, to lead into that root note. These lines often use **scalewise movement** (major, minor, or modal scales) or **chordal arpeggios** (triads or four-part chords).

- Ascending or descending **half-step intervals** are often used, particularly at the end of a measure to connect into the root of the next chord.

With these points in mind, let's take a closer look at how the walking bass line in the preceding example was constructed:

Measure 1	On the Fm7 chord we ascend scalewise (F, G, A♭) within the major scale of the key signature (A♭ major). Then we skip from A♭ to C, which is a partial arpeggio of the Fm7 chord, moving from the 3rd to the 5th. This leads into the root of the next chord (B♭) by whole step.
Measure 2	On the B♭m7 chord we descend scalewise (B♭, A♭, G, F), again within an A♭ major scale. Then we add a half-step connecting tone (F♭, or E) on the "& of 4," which leads into the root of the next chord (E♭) by half step.
Measure 3	On the E♭7 chord we ascend scalewise (E♭, F, G), again within an A♭ major scale. Then we skip from G to B♭, which is a partial arpeggio of the E♭7 chord, moving from the 3rd to the 5th. This leads into the root of the next chord (A♭) by whole step.
Measure 4	On the A♭maj7 chord we ascend scalewise (A♭, B♭, C), again within an A♭ major scale. Then we skip from C to E♭, which is a partial arpeggio of the A♭maj7 chord, moving from the 3rd to the 5th. Then we finally move back to the 3rd of the chord (C) on the "& of 4," leading into the root of the next chord (D♭) by half step.
Measure 5	On the D♭maj7 chord we descend scalewise (D♭, C, B♭, A♭), again within an A♭ major scale. The A♭ leads into the root of the next chord (G) by half step.
Measure 6	On the G7 chord we ascend scalewise (G, A, B), this time within a C major scale. This is because the G7–Cmaj7 chord progression signifies a **momentary key change** to C major. Then we skip from B to D, which is a partial arpeggio of the G7 chord, moving from the 3rd to the 5th. Then we finally add a half-step connecting tone (D♭) on the "& of 4," which leads into the root of the next chord (C) by half step.
Measure 7	On the Cmaj7 chord we descend scalewise (C, B, A, G), continuing within a C major scale.
Measure 8	Continuing on the Cmaj7 chord, we skip from C down to E, which is a partial arpeggio (moving from the root to the 3rd), before ascending within the C major scale (E, F, G).
Measure 9	On the Cm7 chord we descend using a partial four-part chord arpeggio: C (root), B♭ (7th), G (5th). Then we add a half-step connecting tone (G♭) on beat 4, which leads into the root of the next chord (F) by half-step.
Measure 10	On the Fm7 chord we ascend using a four-part chord arpeggio: F (root), A♭ (3rd), C (5th), and E♭ (7th). Then we move back to the 5th of the chord (C) on the "& of 4," leading into the root of the next chord (B♭) by whole step.

Measure 11	On the B♭7 chord we descend using a partial four-part chord arpeggio: B♭ (root), A♭ (7th), F (5th). Then we add a half-step connecting tone (F♭, or E) on beat 4, which leads into the root of the next chord (E♭) by half step.
Measure 12	On the E♭maj7 chord we ascend using a four-part chord arpeggio: E♭ (root), G (3rd), B♭ (5th), and C (6th). Then we move back to the 5th of the chord (B♭) on the "& of 4," leading into the root of the next chord (A♭) by whole step.
Measure 13	On the Abmaj7 chord we ascend using a partial four-part chord arpeggio: A♭ (root), C (3rd), E♭ (5th), and back to C (3rd). Then we add a half-step connecting tone (D♭) on the "& of 4," which leads into the root of the next chord (D) by half step.
Measure 14	On the D7 chord we descend using a four-part chord arpeggio: D (root), C (7th), A (5th), and F♯ (3rd), which leads into the root of the next chord (G) by half step.
Measure 15	On the Gmaj7 chord we ascend scalewise (G, A, B), this time within a G major scale. This is because the D7–Gmaj7 chord progression signifies a **momentary key change** to G major. Then we skip from B to D, which is a partial arpeggio of the Gmaj7 chord, moving from the 3rd to the 5th. Then we finally return to the 3rd (B) on the "& of 4."
Measure 16	Continuing on the Gmaj7 chord, we move from the root (G) down to the 7th (F♯) and back again to the root (G) on beat 3.

Theory note: This song is in the overall key of A♭, but goes through different momentary keys during the song: We have a V–I progression in C major (measures 6–8), a VI–II–V–I–IV progression in E♭ major (measures 9–13), and a V–I progression in G major (measures 14–16). This is typical of jazz standards.

For much more information on analyzing momentary key changes in songs, please refer to my *Contemporary Music Theory, Level Two* book, published by Hal Leonard Corporation.

Next we will add some jazz swing rhythmic comping in the right hand, above this walking bass part in the left hand, as follows:

TRACK 33

Note the jazz swing rhythmic variations in the right hand, again a typical mix of downbeats and upbeats, functioning as rhythmic anticipations. As with the earlier jazz swing examples "in 2," you'll want to get the left-hand pattern on autopilot as much as possible, in order to focus on the rhythmic variations in the right-hand part.

The Jazz-Blues Progression in F

Now we'll learn how to combine the seven-three extended voicings we saw earlier, with a left-hand walking bass part. The vehicle we'll use for this is a 12-bar blues progression in the key of F, a commonly used key for piano-based blues tunes. The basic blues form consists of dominant chords built from the I, IV, and V of the key (henceforth referred to as the I7, IV7, and V7 respectively), as in the following example:

TRACK 34

This is a 12-bar blues sequence, with an extra measure added at the end (measure 13) to return to the tonic chord of F7. The typical 12-bar blues form breaks down into three sections of four bars or measures each:

- The first four measures normally use the I7 (F7 in this case), frequently moving to the IV7 (B♭7 in this case) in the second measure.

- The second four measures (i.e., from measure 5 of the form) begin with the IV7, normally returning to the I7 after two measures (i.e., on measure 7).

- The third four measures (i.e., from measure 9 of the form) begin with the V7 (C7 in this case), typically followed by the IV7 (in measure 10), and then returning to the I7 in measure 11. Measures 11 and 12 are a "turnaround" section leading back to the beginning of the form, and present many chord progression possibilities. The simplest options are to stay on the I7, or to move to the V7 in measure 12—which we do in this example.

There are many variations on this blues chord progression, particularly in jazz blues where more substitutions and complex chords can be used.

We saw earlier that walking bass lines are normally created from scale tones, arpeggios, and half-step connecting lines. On dominant chords in the blues, the scale source most commonly used is the **Mixolydian mode**, built from the root of each chord. This mode is equivalent to a major scale with the 7th degree flatted by half-step. For example, on the F7 chord the bass line can use F Mixolydian, which contains the notes F-G-A-B♭-C-D-E♭ (same as the F major scale except that E is flatted to become E♭). Similarly, on the B♭7 chord the bass line can use B♭ Mixolydian, which contains the notes B♭-C-D-E♭-F-G-A♭ (same as the B♭ major scale except that A is flatted to become A♭), and so on.

With this in mind, let's take a closer look at the walking bass part in Track 34:

Measure 1	On the F7 chord we ascend using a partial four-part chord arpeggio: F (root), A (3rd), and C (5th). Then we add a half-step connecting tone (C♭, or B) on beat 4, which leads into the root of the next chord (B♭) by half step.
Measure 2	On the B♭7 chord we descend scalewise (B♭, A♭, G) within the B♭ Mixolydian mode. Then we add a half-step connecting tone (G♭) on beat 4, which leads into the root of the next chord (F) by half step.
Measure 3	On the F7 chord we ascend using a four-part chord arpeggio: F (root), A (3rd), C (5th), and D (6th).
Measure 4	Continuing on the F7 chord, we begin with the 7th (E♭) and then descend down the arpeggio used in the previous measure. (All the notes in measures 3 and 4 are also contained in the F Mixolydian mode).
Measure 5	On the B♭7 chord we descend scalewise (B♭, A♭, G, F) within the B♭ Mixolydian mode.
Measure 6	Continuing on the B♭7 chord, we skip from B♭ up to D, which is a partial arpeggio (moving from the root to the 3rd) before a series of ascending half steps (D, E♭, E) leading into the root of the next chord (F) by half step.
Measure 7	On the F7 chord we descend scalewise (F, E♭, D, C) within the F Mixolydian mode. Then during beat 4 we have a partial arpeggio, moving from C to A (the 5th to the 3rd of the F7 chord).
Measure 8	Continuing on the F7 chord, we ascend scalewise (F, G, A, B♭) within the F Mixolydian mode, leading into the root of the next chord (C) by whole step.
Measure 9	On the C7 chord we are using a four-part chord arpeggio: C (root) descending to E (3rd), then ascending to G (5th) and A (6th), leading into the root of the next chord (B♭) by half step.

Measures 10–11 Same as for measures 2–3.

Measure 12   On the C7 chord we descend using a four-part chord arpeggio: C (root), B♭ (7th), G (5th), and E (3rd), leading into the root of the next chord (F) by half step.

Next we'll take a closer look at the seven-three extended voicings used in the right hand, in this example:

Measures 1, 3, 7, 11   The 13th of the F7 chord (D) has been added above the 3rd (A). This upgrades the chord to an F13.

Measures 2, 5–6, 10   The 9th of the B♭7 chord (C) has been added above the 7th (A♭). This upgrades the chord to a B♭9.

Measures 4, 8, 13   The 5th of the F7 chord (C) has been added above the 3rd (A).

Measures 9, 12   The 9th of the C7 chord (D) has been added above the 7th (B♭). This upgrades the chord to a C9.

For the jazz pianist, these would be routine upgrades to the dominant chords in this type of jazz-blues progression. Most often the chord symbols are presented as basic dominant 7th chords, and the upgrades are applied at the player's discretion. Notice that there are no alterations (flatted/sharped 5ths or 9ths) in this example, just unaltered upper extensions (9ths and 13ths).

Next we will apply some jazz swing comping rhythms to the right-hand seven-three extended voicings, as follows:

The right-hand voicings are the same as used for Track 34, now with jazz swing comping rhythms added. Practice the left-hand part separately as needed, to help get it on autopilot so that you can again focus on the rhythms and anticipations used in the right hand.

Block (Four-Part) Chord Voicings

Next we'll get into a new voicing technique known as **block voicing**. A block voicing or "shape" results when we use four different pitches within a one-octave range. By this definition, all the four-part chords we saw at the beginning of Chapter 2 qualify as block voicings. In Track 1 we created a II–V–I progression in the key of C, using simple root-position four-part block voicings. In the next example, we will voice lead (move to the closest inversion) between these block voicings, as follows:

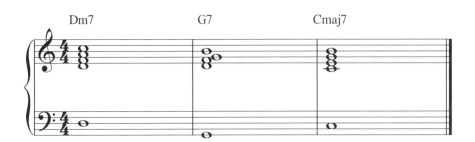

TRACK 36

In comparison to Track 1, notice that the first and last measures are the same, but the second measure now has the G7 chord in second inversion, in order to voice lead smoothly between the successive chords. The top notes move from the 7th on the Dm7 chord, to the 3rd on the G7 chord, and to the 7th on the Cmaj7 chord. This is the same as the seven-three top note voiceleading we first saw in Track 2.

Next we will start with the first Dm7 chord in second inversion, placing the 3rd of the chord on top, voice leading from there as follows:

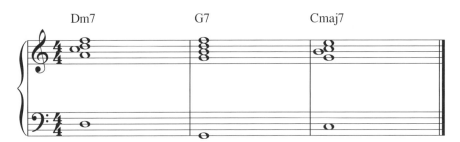

TRACK 37

Now the top notes move from the 3rd on the Dm7 chord, to the 7th on the G7 chord, and to the 3rd on the Cmaj7 chord, the same as the seven-three top note voiceleading in Track 3.

These simple root-3rd-5th-7th block voicings will work OK in many jazz contexts as long as we voice lead appropriately. However, we get a more interesting and sophisticated result by **replacing the root** in the block voicing **with the 9th** of the chord. In other words, in the right hand we can play the 3rd-5th-7th-9th of each chord instead of the root-3rd-5th-7th. This is sometimes referred to as a **"9 for 1" substitution** in the block voicing. Let's see this at work on the same II–V–I progression in C major, now placing the 9th on top of the first Dm9 chord, and voice leading from there as follows:

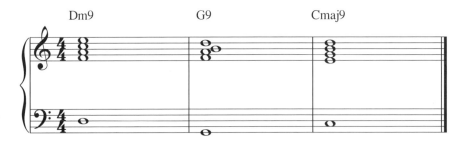

TRACK 38

Note that the chord symbols have now been upgraded to reflect the addition of the 9th to each chord. However, jazz musicians will routinely apply these voicings to spontaneously upgrade more basic II–V–I chord symbols (i.e., Dm7-G7-Cmaj7). The top notes on these voicings now move from the 9th on the Dm9 chord, to the 5th on the G9 chord, and to the 9th on the Cmaj9 chord. In each case, the right-hand block voicing contains the 3rd-5th-7th-9th of each chord.

It is also useful to consider these new 3rd-5th-7th-9th voicings from an upper structure point of view. This is done by looking at the right-hand block voicing as a four-part chord in its own right, with a specific relationship to the root of the overall chord (as defined by the chord symbol). Let's analyze each of the voicings in Track 38 from this point of view:

Measure 1   The right-hand voicing on the Dm9 chord is an Fmaj7 block shape, built from the 3rd (F) of the Dm9 chord. This Fmaj7 block shape is in root position.

Measure 2   The right-hand voicing on the G9 chord is a Bm7♭5 block shape, built from the 3rd (B) of the G9 chord. This Bm7♭5 block shape is in second inversion, voice leading from the previous measure.

Measure 3   The right-hand voicing on the Cmaj9 chord is an Em7 block shape, built from the 3rd (E) of the Cmaj9 chord. This Em7 block shape is in root position, voice leading from the previous measure.

Another way to look at these block voicings is as a further extension of "seven-three extended" voicings, which, as we have seen, typically add the 5th or 9th to the seven-three of the chord. Here we are adding both the 5th and the 9th to the definitive seven-three voicing for each chord.

Next we will start with the upper Fmaj7 block shape (on the Dm9 chord) in second inversion (placing the 5th of the Dm9 chord on top), voice leading from there as follows:

TRACK 39

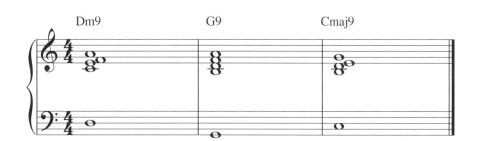

The top notes on these voicings now move from the 5th on the Dm9 chord, to the 9th on the G9 chord, and to the 5th on the Cmaj9 chord. The block voicings are the same as for Track 38, now with the upper Fmaj7 shape (on the Dm9 chord in measure 1) in second inversion, the upper Bm7♭5 shape (on the G9 chord in measure 2) in root position, and the upper Em7 shape (on the Cmaj9 chord in measure 3) in second inversion.

Next we'll explore how to use these new voicings in jazz swing and bossa nova comping styles, with added root-7th intervals in the left hand. We'll begin with a jazz swing rhythmic treatment of the voicings in Track 38 (top notes are the 9th, 5th, and 9th on the Dm9, G9, and Cmaj9 chords respectively):

Swing eighths

TRACK 40

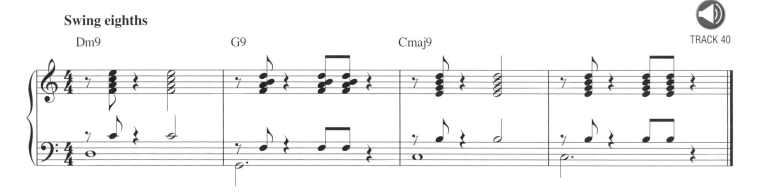

This jazz swing rhythm uses a new left-hand technique of "splitting" the root-7th intervals. The pinky is playing the root of the chord on beat 1 of each measure, sustaining it throughout the measure. Meanwhile the thumb is playing the 7th of the chord with the same rhythm as the right-hand block voicings. This left-hand "split" can be a useful way of adding rhythmic interest to the swing pattern.

Next up is a jazz swing rhythmic treatment of the block voicings in Track 39, transposed up an octave (top notes are the 5th, 9th, and 5th on the Dm9, G9 and Cmaj9 chords respectively):

Swing eighths

TRACK 41

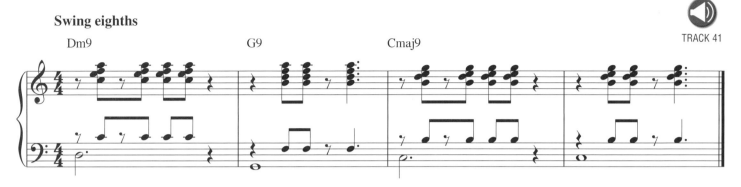

This is a busier jazz swing rhythmic figure compared to Track 40, again using the left-hand "split" of the root-7th intervals.

Now we'll apply some straight-eighths bossa nova comping rhythms to these block voicings, beginning with a bossa nova rhythmic treatment of the voicings and inversions used in Track 38:

TRACK 42

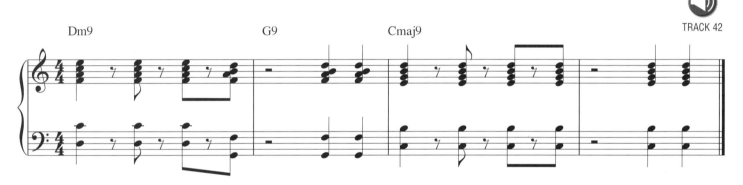

This is a more syncopated bossa nova rhythmic figure compared to earlier examples, with a succession of upbeats (the "& of 2," "& of 3," and "& of 4") being used in measures 1 and 3.

Next up is a bossa nova rhythmic treatment of the block voicings and inversions used in Track 39, again transposed up an octave:

TRACK 43

This busier bossa nova pattern uses successive eighth-note chords on the "& of 2," beat 3, and the "& of 3" in measures 1 and 3, and anticipates beat 3 in measures 2 and 4.

II–V–I Progressions in All Keys (Block Voicings)

Now we'll apply these 3rd-5th-7th-9th (or "9 for 1" substitution) block voicings when playing II–V–I progressions in all keys. We'll be voice leading closely through the changes, as we first saw in Tracks 38 and 39. Our first example in this section starts with the 9th on top of the Dm9 chord in the key of C (as in Track 38), and then voice leads through all of the remaining keys in a Circle of 5ths sequence as follows:

Backing track: (Jazz Swing)

TRACK 44

Note that the left hand is playing a root-7th interval where the range permits, and otherwise is playing the root or root-5th of the chord. Review the text before Track 18 as needed, concerning these left-hand techniques.

On the first II–V–I progression in the key of C, the top notes move from the 9th on the Dm9 chord to the 5th on the G9 chord, and to the 9rd on the Cmaj9 chord (as in Track 38). Then to voice lead closely into the II–V–I progression in the next key of F, the top notes move from the 5th on the Gm9 chord to the 9th on the C9 chord, and to the 5th on the Fmaj9 chord (similar to Track 39, but in the key of F). The top note lines (i.e., 9th-5th-9th and 5th-9th-5th) then alternate around the Circle of 5ths sequence for the remaining keys.

If instead we were to play the first II–V–I progression in C major with the 5th-9th-5th line on top (as in Track 39), then to voice lead properly, the following II–V–I progression in the next key of F would switch to having the 9th-5th-9th line on top. This sequence would then alternate throughout the remaining keys as follows:

(Backing track: Bossa Nova)

TRACK 45

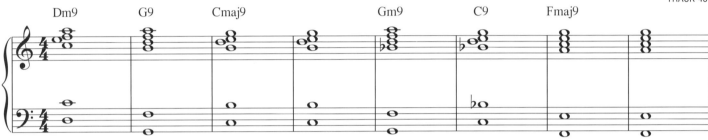

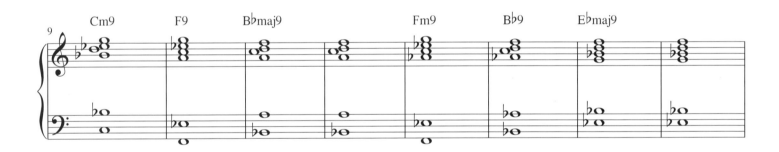

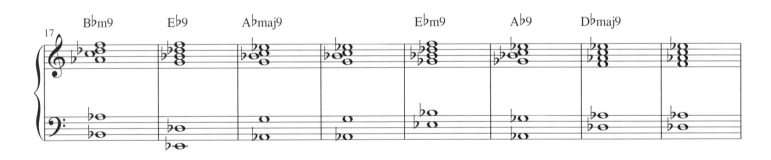

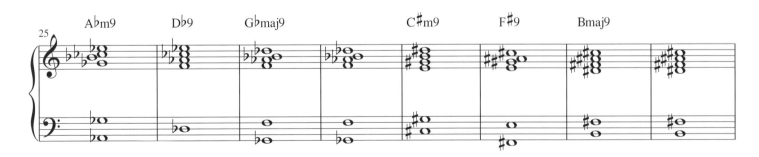

As with the earlier seven-three voicing exercises, once you are comfortable with these II–V–I block voicing exercises in all keys, you should aim to play them from memory (i.e., without reading the notes). Again you can do this by looking at the Circle of 5ths diagram back on page 10, to prompt you for the sequence of keys required.

Next we'll apply comping rhythms to these II–V–I block voicing progressions through all keys, beginning with an example in a **jazz swing** style. This example starts with the 9th on top of the first Dm9 chord, and is based on the block voicings and voice leading that we used in Track 44:

Swing eighths

TRACK 46

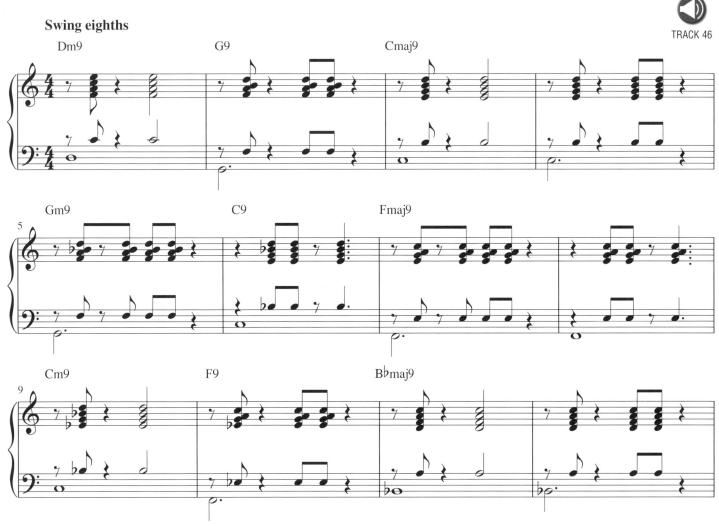

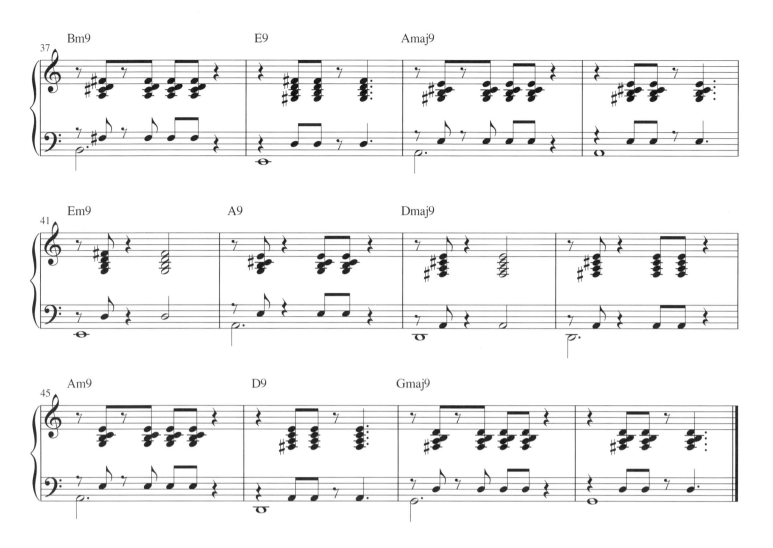

This example uses the left-hand technique of rhythmically "splitting" the root-7th (and root-5th) intervals that we first saw in Track 40.

Our next block voicing example using II–V–I progressions through all the keys is in a **bossa nova** style. This example starts with the 5th on top of the first Dm9 chord, and is based on the voicings and voice leading used in Track 45:

TRACK 47

This example uses the two-measure bossa nova rhythmic phrases from Tracks 42 and 43, repeated throughout all the keys.

Comping through "Just Friends" (Jazz Swing)

Now we'll put these block voicings to work as we "comp through the changes" for the first 16 measures of the well-known jazz standard "Just Friends." All the chord symbols in this example are either major 9ths, minor 9ths, or dominant 9ths, reflecting the five-part chord qualities created when these 3rd-5th-7th-9th block voicings are used. However, as previously noted, jazz pianists often upgrade basic four-part chord symbols with these types of voicings:

All these block voicings are contained in the II–V–I exercises in Tracks 44 and 45. They can also be considered from an **upper structure** point of view, as in the text following Track 38, as follows:

- The right-hand voicings on the major 9th chords are all minor 7th block shapes, built from the 3rd of each chord: Em7 is built from the 3rd of Cmaj9 (measures 1–2 and 17), and Bm7 is built from the 3rd of Gmaj9 (measures 5–6 and 11).

- The right-hand voicings on the minor 9th chords are all major 7th block shapes, built from the 3rd of each chord: E♭maj7 is built from the 3rd of Cm9 (measure 3), D♭maj7 is built from the 3rd of B♭m9 (measure 7), Cmaj7 is built from the 3rd of Am9 (measures 9 and 15), and Gmaj7 is built from the 3rd of Em9 (measure 12).

- The right-hand voicings on the dominant 9th chords are all minor 7♭5th block shapes, built from the 3rd of each chord: Am7♭5 is built from the 3rd of F9 (measure 4), Gm7♭5 is built from the 3rd of E♭9 (measure 8), F♯m7♭5 is built from the 3rd of D9 (measures 10 and 16), C♯m7♭5 is built from the 3rd of A9 (measure 13), and Bm7♭5 is built from the 3rd of G9 (measure 16).

Chapter 4

INTRO TO JAZZ PIANO MELODY TREATMENT

The "Seven-Three Below Melody" Technique

So far, we have explored different techniques for "comping" (accompaniment) on jazz tunes. Now it's time to turn our attention to "melody treatment," i.e., playing the melody of the song in addition to the chord changes. This is typically required in solo piano settings, when there is no other instrument or vocal.

The "seven-three below melody" technique gives you a definitive and stylistically correct way of playing the melodies of jazz standards. This method can be summarized as follows:

- The right hand plays the melody and the seven-three voicing of the chord below the melody at the point of chord change. Melody notes occuring between chord changes are normally played as single notes, without voicings below.

- The left hand plays the root-7th interval (range permitting), root-5th, or root of each chord.

We will first see this process at work with no rhythmic rephrasing of the melody or supporting seven-three voicings, just to become familiar with the overall concept. Afterward, we will explore different rhythmic treatments and phrasing.

The jazz pianist typically will apply these techniques in response to a lead sheet or fake book chart of a song. This shows just the melody and chord symbols, like the following eight-measure example in the style of the classic standard "Autumn Leaves":

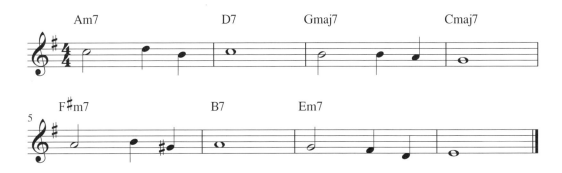

Note that, in order to play the seven-three voicings below the melody in the right hand, we'll need to know these voicings on all the major 7th, minor 7th, and dominant 7th chords, with either the 3rd or the 7th on top. This is because we'll need to fit the seven-three closely below the melody, as these notes are all being played by one hand. Either the 3rd or the 7th will be the closest note to the melody.

This is one reason why the the exercises in Tracks 8–13 showed all the seven-three voicings, with both 3rds and 7ths on top. If you have these exercises under your fingers, this "seven-three below melody" technique will be much easier to play!

Next up is a simple "seven-three below melody" treatment of the preceding lead sheet example:

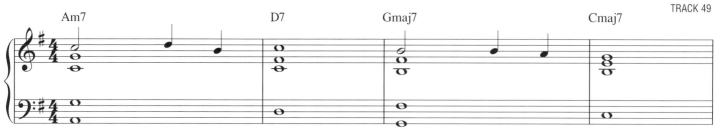

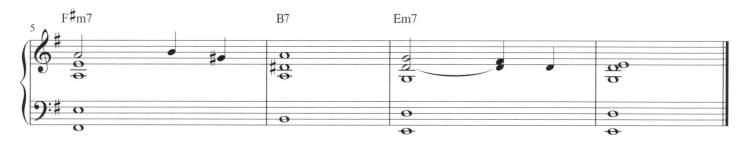

We can make the following observations about the above example:

- The right hand is playing the seven-three of each chord below the melody at the point of chord change (in this case, beat 1 of each measure). Where the chord lasts for more than one measure (measures 7–8), the seven-three voicing is played again on beat 1 of the following measure.

- Because this melody contains a lot of 3rds and 7ths of chords (not unusual in standard tunes), the right-hand voicings look like the "seven-three with doubling" that we first saw in Track 18. However, don't forget that we are just placing the seven-three below the melody, even if the melody is already a 7th or a 3rd.

- In measure 1 on the Am7 chord, the closest seven-three below the C (3rd) in the melody had the 7th on top (G). Then in measure 2 on the D7 chord, the closest seven-three below the C (7th) in the melody had the 3rd on top (F#), and so on. This illustrates the point made earlier, about knowing your seven-three voicings with either the 3rd or 7th on top, as you'll need to play the one closest to the melody in the right hand.

- The left hand is playing the root-7th of the chord where the range permits, in measures 1, 3, 5, 7 and 8. In measures 2, 4, and 6 the left hand is playing only the root of the chord. (Root-5th would have been a possible, but not necessary, option in these measures.)

Let's quickly review the left-hand range limits for the root-7th intervals:

Major 7th intervals *(played on major 7th chords)*	Lowest root note would be F at the bottom of the bass clef, creating the F-E interval.
Minor 7th intervals *(played on minor 7th and dominant 7th chords)*	Lowest root note would be E♭ at the bottom of the bass clef, creating the E♭-D♭ interval.

Now we'll begin to rhythmically rephrase this melody treatment. A simple starting point is to anticipate certain melody notes by moving them an eighth note "to the left." The most obvious candidates for this are melody notes that land on beat 1 of the measure. In the next example, we have taken the melody notes landing on beat 1 of measures 2, 4, 6, and 8, and anticipated them all by an eighth note. For now, we will still play the seven-three voicings below melody, on beat 1 of each measure:

Swing eighths

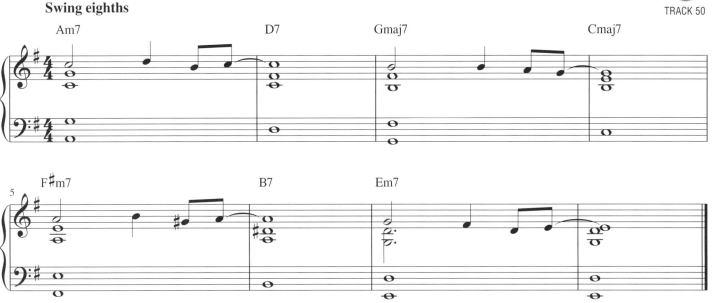

When playing this example, try to get the supporting seven-three voicings as automatic as possible, so you can focus on the rhythmic variations occurring in the melody.

The next version of this example includes rhythmic variations in both the melody and seven-three voicings. The melody now has multiple anticipations, not limited just to beat 1 of the measure. Also, the supporting voicings have some rhythmic rephrasing "in the spaces" between the melody. These voicing patterns are similar to the jazz swing comping rhythms in Chapters 2 and 3, as follows:

Swing eighths

In this example we can see various rhythmic combinations of the melody and supporting seven-three voicings, around beat 1 of each measure as follows:

Measures 1 and 5 — Both the melody and the seven-three voicings are landing on beat 1.

Measures 3 and 7 — The melody is landing on beat 1, and the seven-three voicings are landing on the "& of 1," anticipating beat 2.

Measures 2 and 6	The melody is anticipating beat 1, landing on the "& of 4" of the previous measure, and the seven-three voicings are landing on the "& of 1," anticipating beat 2.
Measures 4 and 8	The melody is anticipating beat 1, landing on the "& of 4" of the previous measure, and the seven-three voicings are landing on beat 2.

Also note that the right-hand seven-three voicings are using the same rhythms as the left-hand part. This creates an effective rhythmic "counterpoint" to the rephrased melody line on top.

This kind of simultaneous rhythmic rephrasing can be a little tricky to execute at first. As you apply these techniques to standards, try rephrasing just the melody first (as in Track 50) before simultaneously rephrasing the melody and supporting voicings (as in Track 51).

Now we'll get some more practice in applying this whole process to a melody. Here's an eight-measure lead sheet example in the style of the famous standard "All the Things You Are":

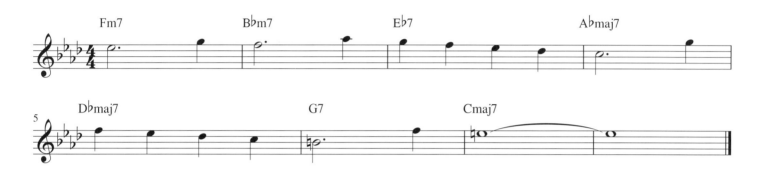

Here's the simple "seven-three below melody" treatment of this example:

TRACK 52

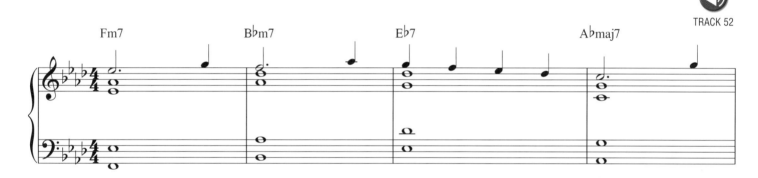

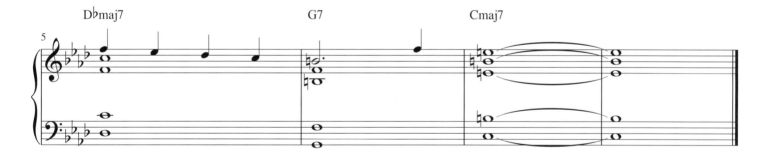

56

Next we have a rhythmic rephrasing of this melody, anticipating the melody notes landing on beat 1 of the even-numbered measures, with the seven-three voicings still landing on the downbeats (similar style to Track 50):

TRACK 53

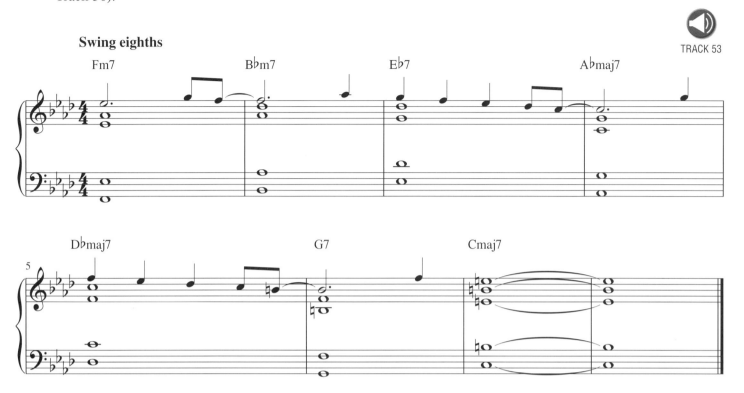

Next we have a more advanced treatment, with multiple anticipations in the melody and rhythmic rephrasing in the supporting voicings, similar style to Track 51:

TRACK 54

This rephrased example includes some new rhythmic techniques, as follows:

- On beat 1 of measures 1, 3, 5, and 7, the melody note and the root of the chord (played with the pinky in each hand) both land on beat 1, and then the inner voices (the 7th in the left hand, and the 3rd and 7th in the right hand) land on the "& of 1." This can be thought of as an extension of the left-hand root-7th "split" technique that we first saw in Track 40.

- In measures 2, 4, and 6, both the melody and supporting voices anticipate beats 1 and 4 of these measures, for a more intense syncopated effect.

Note in measures 7–8: once the melody and root note have been played, we have room for a full two-measure rhythmic "comping" phrase below the melody, similar to the right-hand rhythm used in Track 25. Also, the left-hand part is based entirely on root-7th intervals, except on beat 3 of measure 5, where we briefly have a root-6th (D♭-B♭) interval below the root (D♭) in the melody. This situation is an exception to our normal "seven-three below melody" rules. More about this in the next section.

The Top-Note Voicing Exercise

In this section we have an exercise that will familiarize you with many of the "seven-three below melody" combinations needed when playing the melodies on jazz standards. This will be presented in lead sheet form (melody notes and chord symbols) and contains II–V–I progressions going through all keys in a Circle of 5ths sequence, repeated three times with different melody note combinations each time. After the lead sheet version of the exercise, we'll see a fully voiced version to help you check your playing and voicings.

Before we get into the exercise, there are some important **exception conditions** and **variations** to be aware of when applying the "seven-three below melody" technique. We'll now present each of these, with corresponding music examples taken from the top-note exercise that follows.

Exception Condition 1

If the root is in the melody on a major 7th chord, then the right hand should play a six-three (instead of seven-three) voicing below the melody. This is to avoid the clash occurring between the root in the melody and the 7th of the chord. If the range permits, the left hand can add a root-6th (instead of root-7th) interval in this situation:

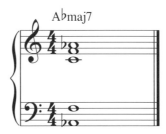

In the above example, the melody note is the root (A♭) on the A♭maj7 chord, so we place the six-three below the melody (F and C) instead of the seven-three (G and C). In the left hand, this is supported by a root-6th interval (A♭-F).

Sometimes this exception condition is indicated by the use of the A♭6 chord symbol, instead of A♭maj7. However, if the major 6th chord symbol is used when the melody is not the root of the chord, it is still possible, and preferable in most jazz situations, to play the seven-three voicing below the melody.

Exception Condition 2

If the 4th or 11th is in the melody on a dominant 7th chord, then the right hand should play a seven-four (instead of seven-three) voicing below the melody. This is to avoid the clash occurring between the 4th/11th in the melody, and the 3rd of the chord. (The presence of the 4th/11th signifies a suspended dominant chord, where the 3rd would not be present.)

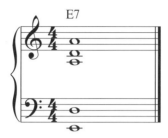

In the above example, the melody note is the 4th/11th (A) on the E7 chord, so we place the seven-four below the melody (D and A) instead of the seven-three (D and G♯). In the left hand, this is supported by a root-7th interval (E-D).

Sometimes this exception condition is indicated by the use of a suspended dominant chord symbol (e.g., E7sus, E9sus, or E11). However, if the E7 chord symbol is used, we need to see ahead of time that the melody is the 4th/11th of the chord, and adjust the voicing accordingly.

Next we'll get into some **variations** that can occur using the seven-three below melody technique. These are different voicing alternatives and preferences, depending on the range and/or which part of the chord is in the melody.

Variation A

If the melody is in the lower part of the treble staff, and if the 3rd of the chord is nearest to the melody, then it is sometimes convenient to do a "7-3 split," where the thumb of the right hand plays the 3rd below the melody, and the thumb of the left hand plays the 7th below. This is not a new voicing as such, just a redistribution of the seven-three voicing between the hands, rather than playing the seven-three entirely in the right hand.

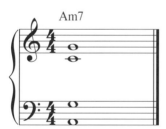

In the above example, the 3rd (C) of the Am7 chord is played by the right-hand thumb (below the melody note G), and the 7th (G) is played by the left-hand thumb (above the root A).

This variation is useful in certain voice leading situations, where it may reduce the hand position movement between successive chord voicings, for example within a II–V–I progression.

Variation B

If the melody is at the bottom of the treble staff (on or below the E above middle C), and if the melody is already the 3rd or 7th of the chord, then in the right hand it is sufficient to play whichever of the 3rd or 7th is missing, below the melody (i.e., place the 3rd below the 7th, or the 7th below the 3rd, rather than place the complete seven-three below melody in the right hand).

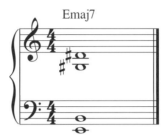

In the above example, the melody note is the 7th (D♯) on the Emaj7 chord, and is at the bottom of the treble staff, so we just place the third (G♯) below the melody instead of the seven-three below, to avoid doubling the 7th too low in the bass register. In the left hand, this is supported by a root-5th interval (E-B). Adding the 5th here is entirely optional; simply playing the root in the left hand would have been fine also.

This variation overlaps with Exception Condition 2, in that we will sometimes have dominant chords with the 4th/11th as a low-register melody note. In this case, the right hand will just play the 7th below the 4th/11th in the melody, as follows:

In the above example, the melody note is the 11th (E) on the B7 chord, and is at the bottom of the treble staff, so we just place the seventh (A) below the melody instead of the seven-four below, to avoid doubling the 4th/11th too low in the bass register.

Variation C

If the melody is 4th/11th of a minor 7th chord and is not lower than G above middle C, then there may be two choices of where to play the seven-three below melody in the right hand, depending on the player's right-hand span or stretching ability:

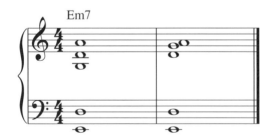

In the above example, the melody note is the 11th (A) on the Em7 chord, and in both measures the seven-three is played below the melody in the right hand. The first measure has a 9th interval stretch in the right hand, with the 7th placed below the melody, and the 3rd placed below the 7th. The second measure has a more compact right-hand voicing, with the 3rd placed right below the 4th/11th in the melody. The breadth and balance of the first voicing is desirable if you are able to reach the 9th interval needed.

However, the second voicing (with the 3rd a whole-step below melody) is OK to use if the first voicing is not practical.

Variation D

If the melody is the root of a minor 7th or dominant 7th chord, then we may choose to play just the 3rd of the chord below the melody, as long as the 7th is being played in the left hand, as part of a root-7th interval. This produces a similar open voicing sound to Variation A, in that the seven-three voicing is split between the thumbs (left hand thumb plays the 7th, right hand thumb plays the 3rd):

If desired, we could still have played seven-three below melody in the right hand, in which case the 7th (A) would have been placed right below the root in the melody. Although the resulting whole-step interval at the top is acceptable, the above voicing has a more open, transparent sound, and is often preferred.

Also, if the root in the melody is high enough in the register, a similar situation to Variation C can occur, where there are two possible ways to fit the seven-three below the melody. The 9th interval stretch, with the 3rd closest to the melody in the right hand, will again sound more open versus the compact sound of placing the 7th immediately below the melody.

Now it's time to look at the top-note exercise in lead sheet form. When playing along with the track, you should try to place seven-three voicings below the melody in the right hand, subject to the exception conditions and variations just outlined. In the left hand, you should go for root-7th intervals if the range permits (review text following Track 49 as needed), otherwise you can play the root or root-5th. Although the rhythms are presented as whole notes, feel free to apply your jazz swing comping rhythms to this exercise as desired.

Top-Note Voicing – Lead Sheet Version

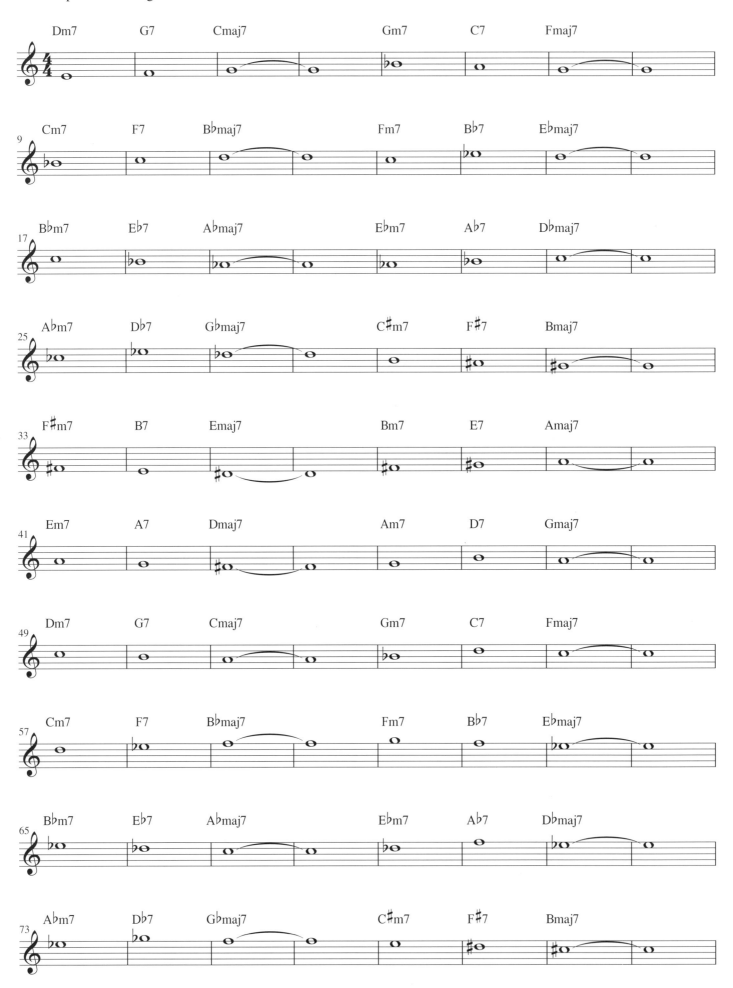

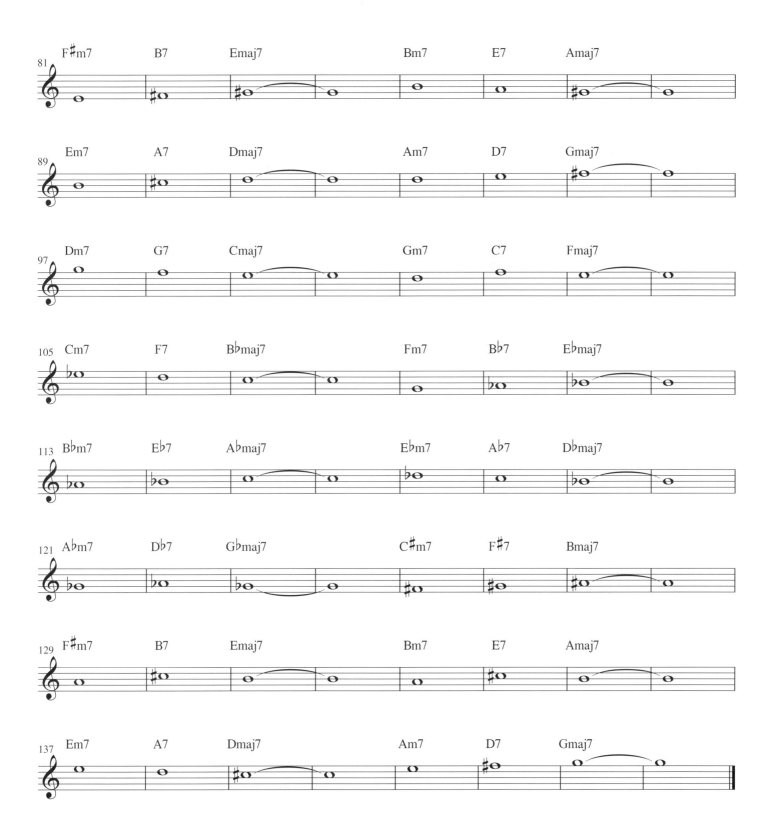

Next up is the fully voiced version of this lead sheet example, showing all the "seven-three below melody" voicings used. After seeing these voicings, we'll also comment on where the exception conditions and variations occurred.

Top-Note Voicing – Fully Voiced Version

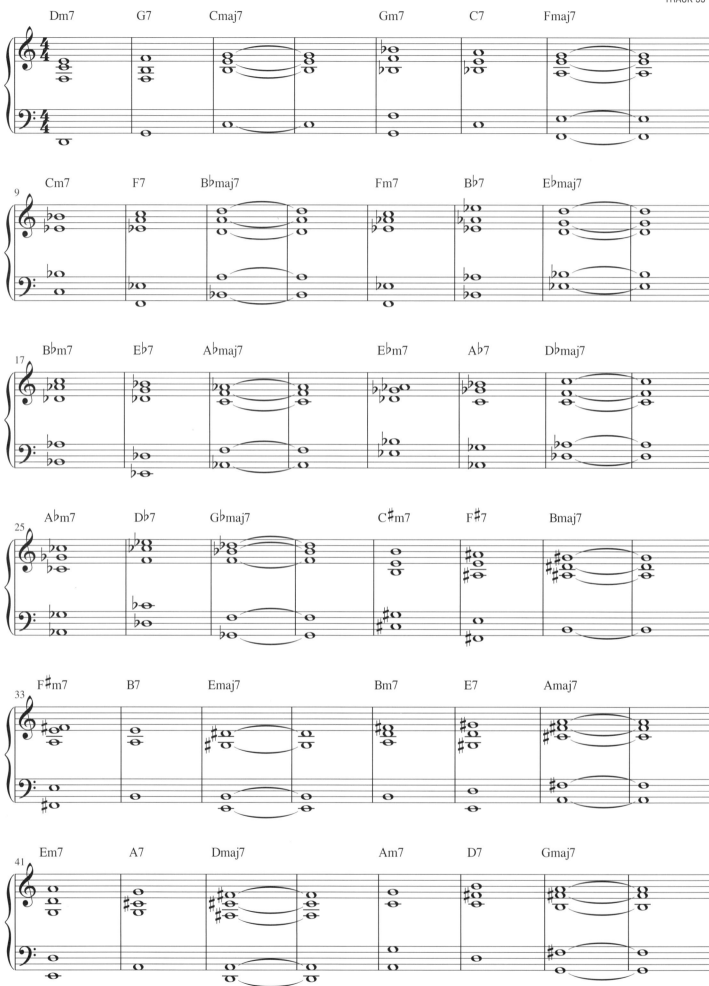

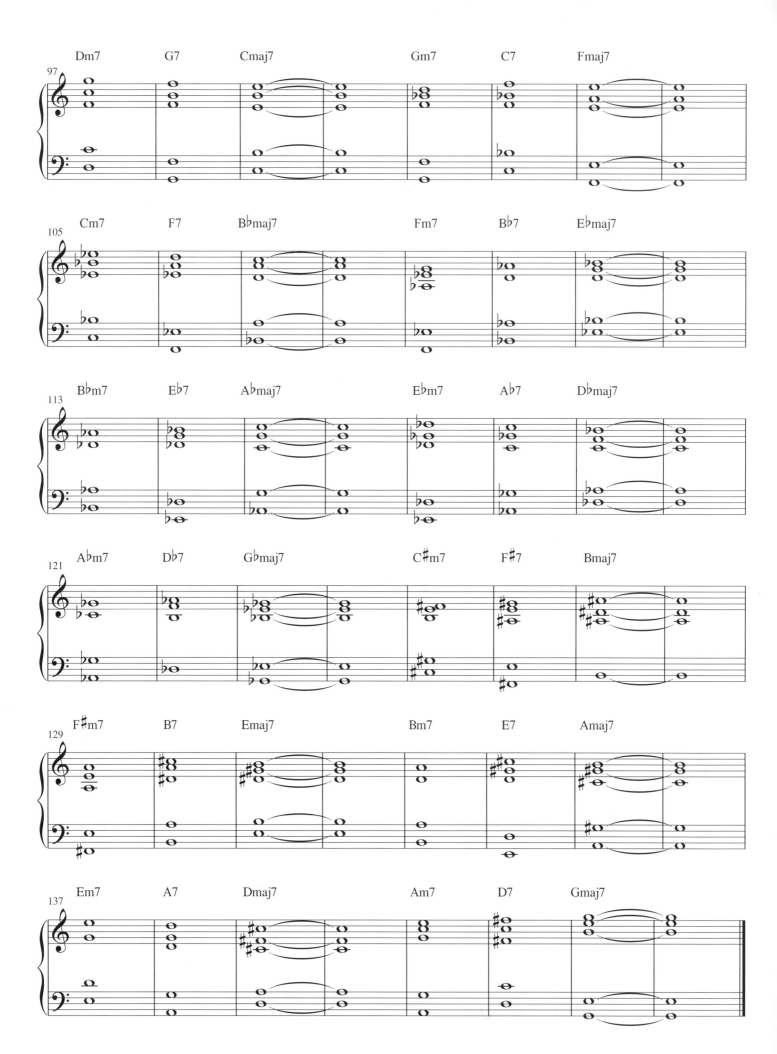

In each measure, we have played seven-three voicings below the melody in the right hand, and root-7th or root-5th intervals (or just the root) in the left hand, subject to the following **exception conditions** and **variations** that occurred:

Measure 9	Variation A occurred on the Cm7 chord, with the seven-three voices split between the hands. This enables the right hand to move more smoothly to the next F7 voicing.
Measure 14	Exception Condition 2 occurred on the B♭7 chord: the 4th/11th (E♭) is in the melody. The seven-four voicing (A♭ and E♭) was played below the melody in the right hand.
Measures 19–20	Exception Condition 1 occurred on the A♭maj7 chord: the root (A♭) is in the melody. The six-three voicing (F and C) was played below the melody in the right hand, and the root-6th (A♭ and F) was played in the left hand.
Measure 34	Exception Condition 2 occurred on the B7 chord: the 4th/11th (E) is in the melody. As the melody is low on the treble staff, the right hand doesn't have room to play the seven-four below the melody. Therefore Variation B also applies, with just the 7th being played below the 4th/11th in the right hand.
Measures 35–36	Variation B occurred on the Emaj7 chord, with just the 3rd (G♯) being placed below the 7th (D♯) in the right hand, instead of the full seven-three voicing. The melody is too low for the 7th to be doubled an octave lower.
Measures 39–40	Exception Condition 1 occurred on the Amaj7 chord: the root (A) is in the melody. The six-three voicing (F♯ and C♯) was played below the melody in the right hand, and the root-6th (A and F♯) was played in the left hand.
Measure 41	Variation C occurred on the Em7 chord, with a 9th interval stretch in the right hand. The 7th (D) was placed below the melody, then the 3rd (G) was placed below the 7th. If this stretch is not practical, you can simply place the 3rd (G) right below the melody.
Measure 45	Variation A occurred on the Am7 chord, with the seven-three voices split between the hands. This enables the right hand to move more smoothly to the next D7 voicing.
Measures 63–64	Exception Condition 1 occurred on the E♭maj7 chord: the root (E♭) is in the melody. The six-three voicing (C and G) was played below the melody in the right hand, and the root-6th (E♭ and C) was played in the left hand.
Measure 65	Variation C occurred on the B♭m7 chord, with a 9th interval stretch in the right hand. The 7th (A♭) was placed below the melody, then the 3rd (D♭) was placed below the 7th. If this stretch is not practical, you can simply place the 3rd (D♭) right below the melody.
Measure 74	Exception Condition 2 occurred on the D♭7 chord: the 4th/11th (G♭) is in the melody. The seven-four voicing (C♭ and G♭) was played below the melody in the right hand.
Measure 81	Variation A occurred on the F♯m7 chord, with the seven-three voices split between the hands. This enables the right hand to move more smoothly to the next B7 voicing.
Measure 85	Variation D occurred on the Bm7 chord, with just the 3rd (D) being placed below the root (B) in the right hand, for a more open sound. This is OK as long as the left hand thumb is playing the 7th (A). Adding the 7th right below the melody would also be OK.
Measures 91–92	Exception Condition 1 occurred on the Dmaj7 chord: the root (D) is in the melody. The six-three voicing (B and F♯) was played below the melody in the right hand, and the root-6th (D and B) was played in the left hand.
Measure 93	Variation C occurred on the Am7 chord, with a 9th interval stretch in the right hand. The 7th (G) was placed below the melody, then the 3rd (C) was placed below the 7th. If this stretch is not practical, you can simply place the 3rd (C) right below the melody.

Measure 97	Variation C occurred on the Dm7 chord, with a 9th interval stretch in the right hand. The 7th (C) was placed below the melody, then the 3rd (F) was placed below the 7th. If this stretch is not practical, you can simply place the 3rd (F) right below the melody.
Measure 102	Exception Condition 2 occurred on the C7 chord: the 4th/11th (F) is in the melody. The seven-four voicing (B♭ and F) was played below the melody in the right hand.
Measure 110	Variation A occurred on the B♭7 chord, with the seven-three voices split between the hands. This enables the right hand to move more smoothly to the next E♭maj7 voicing.
Measure 113	Variation A occurred on the B♭m7 chord, with the seven-three voices split between the hands. This enables the right hand to move more smoothly to the next E♭7 voicing.
Measure 121	Variation A occurred on the A♭m7 chord, with the seven-three voices split between the hands. This enables the right hand to move more smoothly to the next D♭7 voicing.
Measures 123–124	Exception Condition 1 occurred on the G♭maj7 chord: the root (G♭) is in the melody. The six-three voicing (E♭ and B♭) was played below the melody in the right hand, and the root-6th (G♭ and E♭) was played in the left hand.
Measure 133	Variation A occurred on the Bm7 chord, with the seven-three voices split between the hands. This enables the right hand to move more smoothly to the next E7 voicing.
Measure 137	Variation D occurred on the Em7 chord, with just the 3rd (G) being placed below the root (E) in the right hand, for a more open sound. This is OK as long as the left hand thumb is playing the 7th (D). Adding the 7th right below the melody would also be OK.
Measure 138	Exception Condition 2 occurred on the A7 chord: the 4th/11th (D) is in the melody. The seven-four voicing (G and D) was played below the melody in the right hand.
Measures 143–144	Exception Condition 1 occurred on the Gmaj7 chord: the root (G) is in the melody. The six-three voicing (E and B) was played below the melody in the right hand, and the root-6th (G and E) was played in the left hand.

Familiarity with this exercise is a great preparation for playing melodies of jazz standards with the "seven-three below melody" technique. Grab that fake book and start playing!

The "Block Voicing Below Melody" Technique

Our next melody treatment technique uses block voicings in the left hand, below a single-note melody in the right hand. In Chapter 3 we saw that block voicings consisted of four different pitches within a one-octave range, and we played them in the right hand when comping. Now we'll see how to play them in the left hand, while supporting a right-hand melody. For this to be effective, the left-hand voicings need to be around the middle C area, which may require the right-hand melody to be transposed up an octave in some cases.

We also saw in Chapter 3 that if we replaced the root of the chord with the 9th in the block voicing, playing the 3rd-5th-7th-9th of the chord, this resulted in a more sophisticated sound compared to simply using the basic root-3rd-5th-7th of the chord. So we will explore this option when forming left-hand block voicings to support the melody.

We will first see this "block voicing below melody" technique with no rhythmic rephrasing of the melody or supporting block voicings, just to become familiar with the overall concept. Afterward, we will explore different rhythmic treatments and phrasing.

As with the preceding seven-three below melody technique, the jazz pianist will typically apply this block voicing technique in response to a lead sheet or fake book chart of a song. This will show just the melody and chord symbols, like the following 16-measure example in the style of the classic standard "Just Friends":

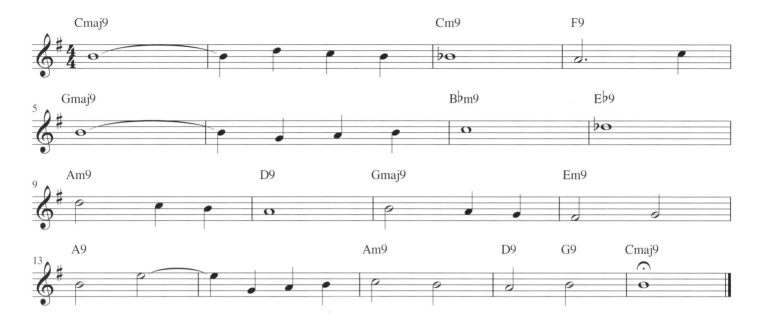

First of all, we'll place the block voicings in the left hand, below the melody shown here in the right hand, without rhythmic rephrasing or embellishment. The left hand is playing 3rd-5th-7th-9th block voicings on each chord around the middle C area, and voice leading (moving by close intervals) from one measure to the next:

TRACK 56

The roots of the chord are not being played in this example. The term "rootless voicing" is sometimes used to describe this technique. In a jazz band situation, the root is normally provided by the bass player, as you can hear on Track 56. However, the above example still works as a solo piano voicing technique, because mainstream jazz styles don't require the root of the chord in order to be "definitive," unlike pop or rock styles. The 3rd and 7th of each chord, present in all the above block voicings, are sufficient to define each chord to our ear.

These block voicings can also be considered from an upper structure point of view, as follows:

- The left-hand voicings on the major 9th chords are all minor 7th block shapes, built from the 3rd of each chord: Em7 is built from the 3rd of Cmaj9 (measures 1–2 and 17), and Bm7 is built from the 3rd of Gmaj9 (measures 5–6 and 11).

- The left-hand voicings on the minor 9th chords are all major 7th block shapes, built from the 3rd of each chord: E♭maj7 is built from the 3rd of Cm9 (measure 3), D♭maj7 is built from the 3rd of B♭m9 (measure 7), Cmaj7 is built from the 3rd of Am9 (measures 9 and 15), and Gmaj7 is built from the 3rd of Em9 (measure 12).

- The left-hand voicings on the dominant 9th chords are all minor 7♭5th block shapes, built from the 3rd of each chord: Am7♭5 is built from the 3rd of F9 (measure 4), Gm7♭5 is built from the 3rd of E♭9 (measure 8), F#m7♭5 is built from the 3rd of D9 (measures 10 and 16), C#m7♭5 is built from the 3rd of A9 (measure 13), and Bm7♭5 is built from the 3rd of G9 (measure 16).

These block voicings and upper structure relationships are the same as for the right-hand part in Track 48, now played in the left hand in a lower register, and using different inversions and voice leading, and with no rhythmic rephrasing as yet.

Now we'll look at rhythmically rephrasing this melody treatment. As with the previous "seven-three below melody" examples, we'll start with some melody anticipations in the right hand, while still playing the accompanying voicings on the downbeats. In the next example, we have just a couple of melody anticipations in measures 1–8, and then a busier series of anticipations in measures 9–16:

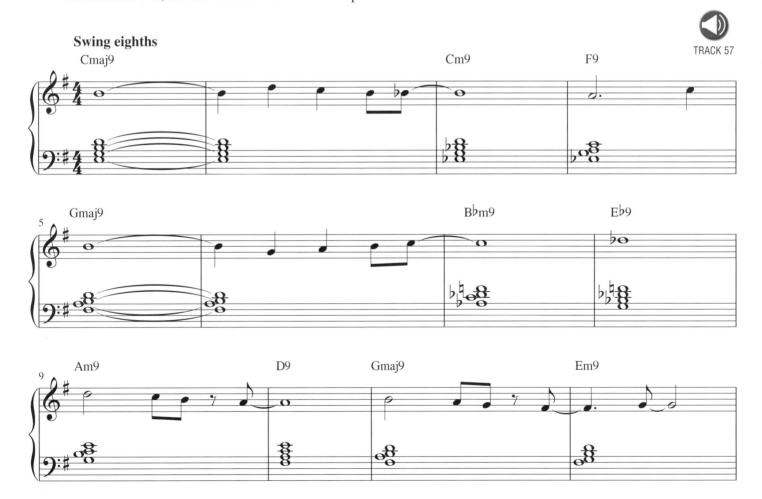

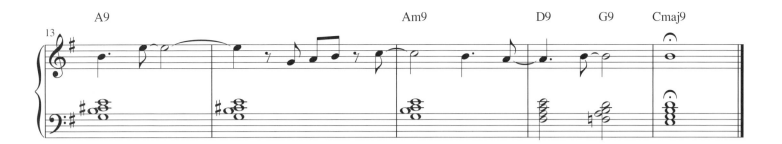

Note how the right-hand rhythmic rephrasing is building during this example. In the first half (measures 1–8), we have only anticipations of beat 1 in measures 3 and 7. Starting in measure 9, we then build up with anticipations of beat 1 (measures 10, 12, 15, and 16), beat 3 (measures 12, 13, and 16), and beat 4 (measures 9, 11, and 14). This busier rhythmic rephrasing is typical of mainstream jazz and swing styles.

Our final example in this chapter combines some more intense rhythmic rephrasing in the right-hand melody with rephrased rhythms in the left-hand block voicings. Sometimes the left-hand rhythms will be "in the spaces" between the melody, and sometimes the phrases will be "concerted," with both hands playing together:

TRACK 58

The right-hand rephrasing now includes some "delayed" as well as "anticipated" melody notes, in comparison to the melody lead sheet prior to Track 56. For example, let's look at the melody treatment in measure 2 in more detail:

- The melody note D on beat 2 of the original lead sheet is now delayed until beat 3.

- The melody note C on beat 3 of the original lead sheet is now delayed until the "& of 3".

- The melody note B on beat 4 of the original lead sheet stays on beat 4.

- The melody note B♭ on beat 1 (measure 3) of the original lead sheet is now anticipated and lands on the "& of 4" in measure 2.

Essentially, this phrase has all been squeezed into the last half of measure 2, with four consecutive eighth notes ending with an anticipation. This also occurs in measures 6 and 14, and again is typical of jazz swing rephrasing. Elsewhere, the right hand is often anticipating beats 1 and/or 3, and sometimes beat 4 of the measure.

Note that the left hand is either playing jazz swing comping rhythms during sustained notes in the melody (measures 1–6), or playing "concerted" rhythms with the right hand (measures 7–8 and 12–13), or some combination of these. Have fun trying out your own rephrased version of this melody while playing along with the band on Track 58!

Chapter 5

INTRO TO JAZZ PIANO SOLOING

Soloing Techniques for Jazz Standards

Next we'll introduce some techniques for soloing—improvising a solo in the right hand—on jazz standards. Normally, when a jazz band plays a standard, the "head" (main melody of the song) is played at least once, followed by solos from one or more instrumentalists (piano, sax, bass, etc), before returning to play the "head" one or more times to finish the arrangement. When it's your turn to take a solo at the piano, you'll usually be following the form of the song, but improvising your own single-note right-hand part "over the changes." You'll also want to play some left-hand voicings to support (or "comp" below) your right-hand soloing. Here we'll use the left-hand block voicings introduced in the last chapter to support our right-hand solos.

When soloing on a jazz standard, a good starting point is to vary the melody of the song. This can be thought of as a continuation of the melody rephrasing process we began in the last chapter. Following this, we'll make use of techniques such as **neighbor tones**, **arpeggios**, and **target notes** to further extend and personalize your piano solos.

As with the melody treatment techniques in the last chapter, the jazz pianist will typically be soloing in response to a lead sheet or fake book chart of a song. Here's a lead sheet example in the style of the famous standard "A Foggy Day":

We'll start out by simply placing left-hand block voicings below the right-hand melody, as follows:

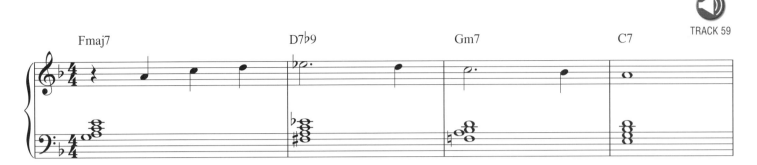

Note that in most cases the left-hand block shapes have upgraded the above chords to 9th chords by using the 3rd-5th-7th-9th of the chord. However, the chord symbols are still shown in their basic 7th or four-part form. This is all typical in mainstream jazz styles. The above example also contains a few left-hand block voicings we haven't seen yet:

Measure 2 We are playing a 3rd-5th-7th-♭9th voicing on the D7(♭9) chord. The left-hand shape is an F♯dim7, built from the 3rd of the overall D7(♭9) chord.

Measures 5, 13 We are playing a root-3rd-5th-6th voicing on the F6 chord. This avoids the tension of placing the 7th of the chord (e.g., in a 3rd-5th-7th-9th voicing) below the root (F) in the melody.

Measure 6 We are playing a root-3rd-5th-7th voicing on the Dm7(♭5) chord.

Our next stage is to begin rephrasing the melody of the song. As well as the anticipations and delayed notes that we saw in Track 58, we'll also add some repeated notes, as follows:

TRACK 60

Note that several of the quarter-note melody phrases from the lead sheet have been squeezed into eighth-note phrases, using anticipations and delayed notes. For example, in measure 1 on the lead sheet we have the melody notes A, C, and D falling on beats 2, 3, and 4 respectively. These have been squeezed into one and a half beats on the rephrased version, with the A being delayed until the "& of 2," and the D moved earlier on to the "& of 3," anticipating beat 4.

Beat 1 of measure 2 is then also anticipated, with the E♭ being moved earlier on to the "& of 4" in measure 1. We also now have some repeated notes: this E♭ is then repeated later in measure 2, the C anticipating beat 1 of measure 3 is repeated later in measure 3, and so on. These are all typical jazz rephrasings that can be part of a melody interpretation, or a springboard for an improvised solo.

Next, we'll further develop the solo by adding **neighbor tones** around the rephrased melody. Neighbor tones are notes that are adjacent to the melody, either above (**upper neighbor**) or below (**lower neighbor**). Neighbor tones are normally chosen either from the scale corresponding to the key signature (F major in this case), or from a momentary scale if the tune is modulating through different keys, or by simply moving a half-step interval above or below the melody. (The half-step from below is much more common.)

We can normally get away with a half-step lower neighbor, even if that note is **chromatic** (does not belong) to the key or scale, whereas upper neighbors that are **diatonic** (belong) to the key or scale are generally safer to use in mainstream jazz and swing styles. With this in mind, let's look at the next example, which adds upper and lower neighbor tones in the right hand, together with some rhythmic rephrasing in the left-hand voicings:

TRACK 61

Note that some of the right-hand phrases from Track 60 have now been embellished with upper and lower neighbor tones. For example, after the E♭ that anticipates beat 1 of measure 2, we move up to F (upper neighbor), down to D (lower neighbor), and then back to E♭ for the anticipation of beat 3. Similarly, after the C that anticipates beat 1 of measure 3, we move down to B♭ (lower neighbor), up to D (upper neighbor), and then back to C for the anticipation of beat 3, and so on.

The left-hand block voicings are now frequently anticipating beat 1, together with the rephrased rhythms in the right hand. Elsewhere, the left hand uses typical jazz swing rhythms in the spaces between the right-hand lines, for example in measures 4 and 8.

Now we'll kick the solo up another notch by using **arpeggios** and **target notes**. A target note is a note within a chord that is a desirable landing point during the solo, when played over the chord. A series of target notes therefore gives us a framework around which a solo can be developed. In jazz styles, we can use chord tones and extensions for target notes, i.e., the root, 3rd, 5th, 7th, 9th, 11th, and/or 13th of the chord. Depending on the chord symbol and context, we may also have an altered 5th (♭5 or ♯5) on major, minor, or dominant chords, and an altered 9th (♭9 or ♯9) on dominant chords. These altered 5ths/9ths make particularly good target notes, as they have a lot of color and character. One target note per measure is a good starting point for this approach, and this may be varied depending on the chord rhythms and/or tempo of the song.

In order to flesh out the solo, beyond just having the target notes, we can add connecting tones in between. A common way of doing this in mainstream jazz styles is to use arpeggios within each chord, i.e., playing individual chord tones in a "broken chord" style. In the following example, we have chosen a target note on each chord, then connected between these successive target notes using arpeggios within each chord:

The preceding example contains a left-hand block voicing variation we haven't seen yet:

Measure 7   We are playing a 7th-9th-3rd-13th voicing on the G7 chord, upgrading it to a G13 chord. The left-hand shape is an Fmaj7♭5, built from the 7th of the overall G7 chord.

The target notes on each chord are indicated below the treble staff in Track 62. For example, in the first measure the target note on beat 1 is E, the 7th of the Fmaj7 chord. Then in the second measure, the target note on the D7♭9 chord is anticipated, landing on the "& of 4" in measure 1 and tied over to beat 1 of measure 2. This target note is E♭, the ♭9th of the D7♭9 chord. Similarly, the target note on the Gm7 chord is anticipated, landing on the "& of 4" in measure 2 and tied over to beat 1 of measure 3. This target note is D, the 5th of the Gm7 chord, and so on. There are many choices for target notes of course. To start with, you'll want to move between target notes by smaller intervals, mostly 2nds and 3rds, to give the resulting target line a more melodic character. Feel free to experiment!

In between each target note, we have used arpeggios on each chord. For example, after the target note E (7th) on the Fmaj7 chord in measure 1, we then play the 9th (G), 3rd (A), and 5th (C) of the chord. These notes collectively form a 3rd-5th-7th-9th block shape on the Fmaj7 chord, equivalent to building an Am7 four-part upper structure from the 3rd of the chord. Similarly, after the target note Eb (♭9th) on the D7♭9 chord anticipating beat 1 of measure 2, we then play the 3rd (F♯), 5th (A), and 7th (C) of the chord. These notes collectively form a 3rd-5th-7th-♭9th block shape on the D7♭9 chord, equivalent to building an F♯dim7 four-part upper structure from the 3rd of the chord. Most of the remaining measures use a similar arpeggio technique on each chord, except for measure 11, which uses a scalewise connecting run (F-G-A-B♭) derived from the major scale of the key signature (F major).

Soloing Techniques for Jazz-Blues

Track 62 is a very good example of **playing through the changes**, where we are choosing target notes and arpeggios on a chord-by-chord basis when soloing. However, jazz and jazz-blues solos can also be created by **playing over the changes**. This is done by staying within a "scale source" related to the key of the song, instead of hitting different target notes relating to each chord. The most common scale used for this purpose in mainstream jazz and jazz-blues styles is the blues scale. Let's start out by reviewing the notes in a C blues scale, as follows:

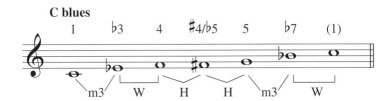

The intervals between successive scale degrees are shown below the staff: minor 3rd, whole step, half step, half step, minor 3rd, and whole step. Also the intervals between each note and the tonic of the scale (C) are shown above the staff: minor 3rd, perfect 4th, augmented 4th/diminished 5th, perfect 5th, and minor 7th.

For further information on intervals and definitions of all interval relationships, please refer to my *Contemporary Music Theory, Level One* or *All About Music Theory* books, published by Hal Leonard Corporation.

For further information on building blues and pentatonic scales, please refer to my *Contemporary Music Theory, Level Two* or *All About Music Theory* books, published by Hal Leonard Corporation.

The easiest way to begin using a blues scale for soloing over the changes is to work with a 12-bar blues chord progression. Here's a basic 12-bar blues "chord chart" in the key of C:

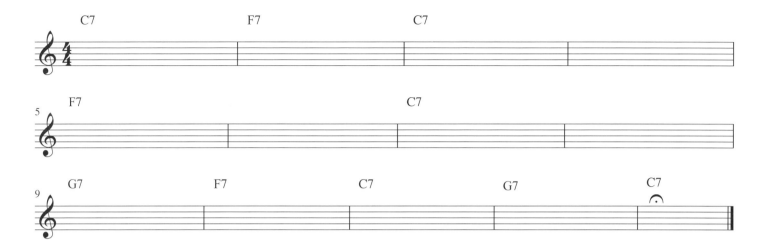

In this case, we have followed the 12-bar blues form with a single ending measure of C7 (measure 13). Review the text following Track 34 as needed, regarding how the 12-bar blues form is constructed.

On to our next soloing example, which uses the C blues scale over the above 12-bar blues progression in C. This example also intruduces some new "seven-three extended" voicings, now played in the left hand:

Swing eighths

TRACK 63

Note that the solo uses only notes within the C blues scale over the different chords, and that the solo essentially consists of three four-measure phrases, consistent with how the blues form is constructed.

The "seven-three extended" voicings that we first saw as a right-hand comping device in Chapter 3 (and in particular on the jazz-blues progression in Track 34) are now being used in the left hand to support the right-hand solo. In order for this to work, the left hand has to play around the middle C area—too low and these voicings will sound muddy, too high and they will lack definition and get in the way of the right-hand solo.

Back in Track 34, the seven-three extended voicings were adding unaltered chord tones/extensions to the dominant chords: either the 5th, 9th, or 13th was added. This is also happening in Track 63: for example, the 13th of the F7 chord (D) has been added above the 3rd (A) in measures 2, 5–6, and 10, and the 9th of the C7 chord (D) has been added above the 7th (B♭) in measure 13. However, we are now also adding alterations to some of the dominant chords, as follows:

Measures 1, 3–4, 7–8, 11   The ♯9th of the C7 chord (D♯ or E♭) has been added above the 7th (B♭). This upgrades the chord to a C7(♯9).

Measures 9 and 12   The ♯5th of the G7 chord (D♯ or E♭) has been added above the 3rd (B). This upgrades the chord to a G7♯5 or G7♭13.

These dominant alterations work, in part because the added note (E♭) is a prominent "blue note" within the C blues scale, so these alterations reinforce the "blues feeling" of this example. Again note that the chord symbols are still shown as basic dominant 7th chords, with the alterations being applied at the player's discretion.

Note that while the sharped 9th of the C7 chord would technically be described as D♯, it is shown in this example as E♭ for consistency with the C blues scale. The sharped 5th of the G7 chord, also technically described as D♯, is shown as E♭ for the same reason. The sharped 5th is equivalent to the flatted 13th on the dominant chord—i.e., the chord symbols G7♯5 and G7♭13 are equivalent and mean the same thing.

Our next soloing example uses the **relative minor blues** scale over the same C blues progression. We'll need to review a bit of theory here: the minor key that shares the same key signature as a major key is known as the relative minor of that major key. The relative minor always starts on the 6th degree of the corresponding major scale. The key signature of the previous example (Track 63) had no sharps and no flats. This key signature works for both C major and its relative minor, A minor (A is the 6th degree of a C major scale.)

For further information on key signatures and relative minor concepts, please refer to my *Contemporary Music Theory, Level One* or *All About Music Theory* books, published by Hal Leonard Corporation.

The most common blues scales to use when soloing **over the changes** are as follows:

- The blues scale built from the tonic of the major key (i.e., using a C blues scale over the C blues progression, as in Track 63)

- The blues scale built from the relative minor of the major key (i.e., using an A blues scale over the C blues progression, as in Track 64, which we'll see shortly)

Before we get to the next example, let's briefly review the notes in an A blues scale, as follows:

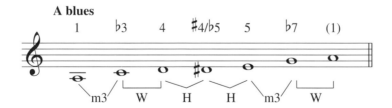

Again, the intervals between successive notes in the scale, and between the tonic (A) and the other notes in the scale, are shown below and above the staff respectively.

Here then is the next example, soloing with the A blues scale over the same C blues progression, and introducing some grace note embellishments in the right hand:

Swing eighths

This solo uses notes within the A blues scale over the different chords and consists of three four-measure phrases. Grace notes are used to connect the half steps within the A blues scale (i.e., between D and D#/Eb, and between D#/Eb and E) in measures 3–4, 7, and 9. Additionally, a whole-step grace note connects the G and A in measure 11.

This example again uses seven-three extended voicings in the left hand—adding no alterations this time, just some unaltered upper extensions: the 13th of the F7 chord (D) and the 9th of the C7 (D) have been added as in Track 63, and the 13th of the G7 chord (E) has been added above the 3rd (B) in measures 9 and 12. Again, the left-hand rhythmic phrasing used to support the right-hand solo is typical of jazz swing and jazz-blues styles.

Our last solo example combines phrases from both the C blues and A blues scales over the same C blues progression, this time adding eighth-note triplet figures for a busier, more intense effect:

TRACK 65

Swing eighths

Note the mix of C blues scale and A blues scale phrases used in this solo. For example, in measure 1 on the C7 chord, the solo phrase comes from the C blues scale, and then in measures 2–4 the solo phrases come from the A blues scale. Similar blues scale "switching" occurs from measure 5 to measures 6–8, and from measure 9 to measures 10–12. This is a great way to add sophistication and interest to your jazz-blues solos! Also, the A blues scale phrases in measures 3, 7, and 11 include an eighth-note triplet subdivision during beat 3, which helps to build the energy of the solo.

The left hand uses a mix of seven-three extended voicings, as follows:

- Adding the ♯9th to the C7 in measures 1 and 11.

- Adding the 13th to the F7 in measures 2, 5–6, and 10.

- Adding the (unaltered) 9th to the C7 in measures 3–4, 7–8, and 13.

- Adding the ♭13th (equivalent of the ♯5th) to the G7 in measure 9 and on the "& of 3" in measure 12.

- Adding the (unaltered) 13th to the G7 in measure 12.

Have fun playing along with all the audio tracks in this soloing chapter. And don't forget to experiment with some improvisation ideas of your own!

For more information on using blues scales when improvising, please see my companion volumes in the Hal Leonard Keyboard Style Series, *Blues Piano: The Complete Guide with CD* and *Jazz-Blues Piano: The Complete Guide with CD*.

Chapter 6
STYLE FILE

In this chapter we have five tunes based on classic jazz standards. The piano parts for these tunes contain a mixture of "comping" or accompaniment, melody treatment, and improvised solo sections. In the comping sections, the right hand is playing either seven-three, seven-three extended, or four-part block voicings. These comping voicings are shown first as half notes or whole notes, then later in the piece they are played with suitable rhythms for the style.

In the melody treatment sections, we are using either the "seven-three below melody" technique in the right hand or playing a single-note melody in the right hand above block voicings in the left hand. In the solo section in tune #5, the left hand is playing seven-three extended voicings below the right-hand solo. When the piano part is comping, either a guitar or flute is playing the melody—except for tune #5, which has just piano comping and soloing sections.

We will also analyze the form of each tune. A common form used in jazz standards is "A A B A," where each of the letters A and B represent eight-measure sections of the song. In this form, the first two "A" sections are substantially similar, followed by a different "B" section, followed by the last "A" section which is similar to the first two sections. Tunes #1 and #4 in this section are based on standards with an "A A B A" form.

Another common form used in jazz standards is "A B C D", where each of the letters A, B, C, and D represent substantially different eight-measure sections of the song. Tunes #2 and #3 in this section are based on standards with an "A B C D" form. By contrast, most blues and jazz-blues tunes use a "12-bar blues" form, as seen earlier in Tracks 34 and 63–65. Tune #5 is based on a 12-bar blues form.

For information purposes, the chord symbols in these tunes have been upgraded to reflect any extensions added (i.e., 9ths or 13ths) by using seven-three extended or block voicing techniques. In practice, however, experienced players typically will apply these upgrades to basic chord symbols (i.e., "seventh" chords) at their discretion.

These tunes are recorded with a band (bass, drums, and comping/melody instruments) as well as piano. On the audio tracks, the band (minus the piano) is on the left channel, and the piano is on the right channel. To play along with the band on these tunes, just turn down the right channel. Slow and Full Speed tracks are provided on the audio for each song (except for tune #4, a slow ballad).

1. Duke's Sweetheart

The first tune is written in the style of "Satin Doll," a classic jazz swing tune by Duke Ellington based on an "A A B A" form. In the first A section (measures 1–8) the piano is comping with basic seven-three voicings as half notes, supporting the guitar melody. In the second A section (measures 9–16), the right hand doubles the top note of the seven-three voicings one octave lower, and both hands are playing jazz swing rhythms with anticipations. Then in the first B section (measures 17–24), the right hand uses some seven-three extended voicings (adding 5ths and 9ths to the chords), while the left hand is adding some root-7th intervals.

In the next A section (measures 25–32), the piano returns to half-note rhythms, this time with block voicings in the right hand over root notes in the left hand. All these block voicings contain the 3rd-5th-7th-9th of each chord, equivalent to building a four-part upper shape from the 3rd of each chord. Although we are now at the end of the regular "A A B A" form, in this arrangement we added an extra A section (measures 33–40) so that the piano can play these block voicings with some jazz swing rhythms, and with some root-7th intervals added in the left hand. Finally, we have a Coda section (measures 41–47), which is essentially a "tag," repeating the last four measures of the A section two more times for a final ending.

In the jazz swing comping sections, make sure that you "swing the eighths" correctly and observe the rests. Also use the sustain pedal sparingly (if at all) in these sections, as it can detract from the swing feel needed. When you are comfortable with all the voicings, go ahead and improvise your own comping rhythms over these classic changes!

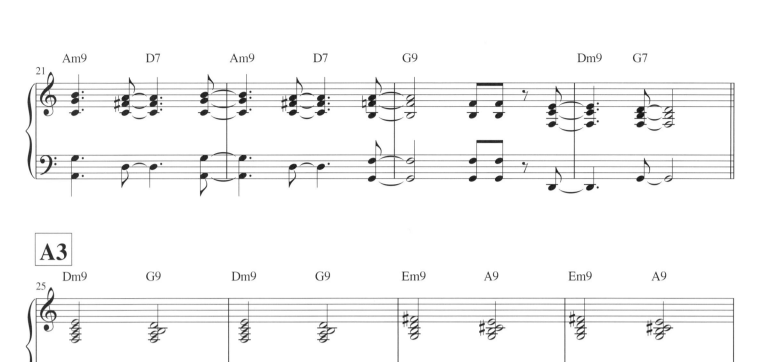

A3

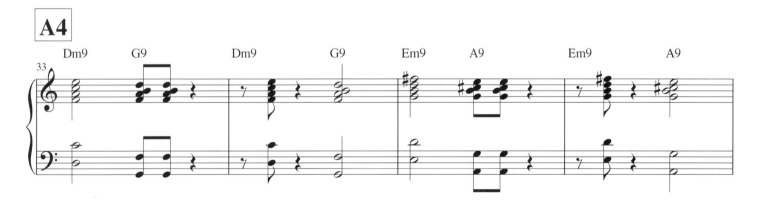

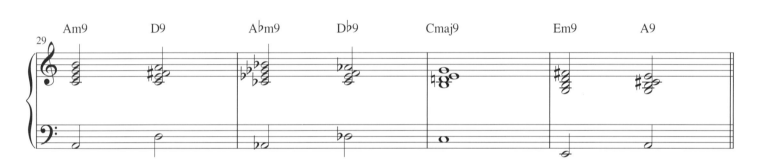

A4

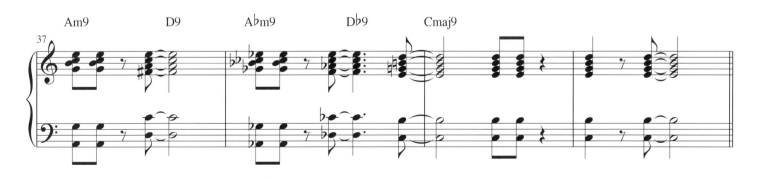

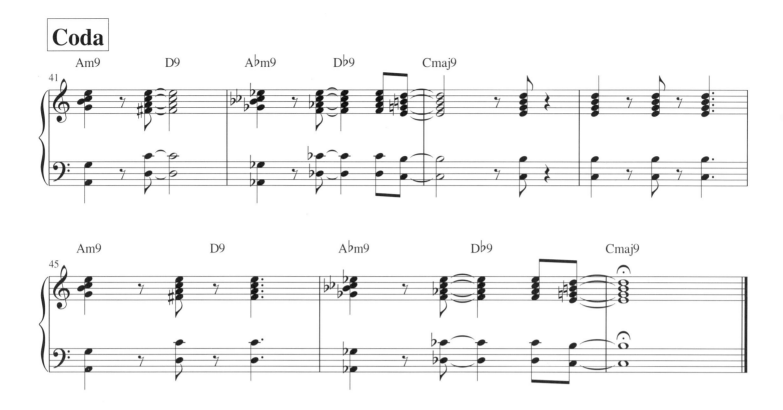

2. Carnival Time

Next we have a tune written in the style of "Black Orpheus," a classic bossa nova tune by Louis Bonfi based on an "A B C D" form. In the first A and B sections (measures 1–16), the piano comping uses seven-three voicings with octave doubling, supporting the flute melody with half-note and whole-note rhythms. In the first C and D sections (measures 17–32), both hands are now applying bossa nova comping rhythms to the same seven-three voicings. Then in the second A and B sections (measures 33–48), the piano part returns to half-note and whole-note rhythms, supporting the organ solo with four-part block shapes in the right hand (except for the Dm "octave doubled" triad built from the 3rd of the Bm7♭5 chord in measures 34 and 36) over some root-7th and root-5th intervals in the left hand. Finally, in the last C and D sections (measures 49–65), both hands are now applying busier bossa nova comping rhythms to the same block voicings.

Make sure you are "in the pocket" with the straight-eighths rhythmic subdivisions and anticipations in the C and D sections. As with the jazz swing styles, observe the rests and use the sustain pedal sparingly (if at all) in these sections, for a cleaner and more stylistic effect.

3. Stella by Candlelight

Our next tune is written in the style of "Stella by Starlight," one of the most performed and recorded jazz standards of all time. This classic song was written by Victor Young, using an "A B C D" form. In this example, we are playing a melody treatment, using the "seven-three below melody" technique in the right hand. Here is a lead sheet, showing the melody and chord symbols, the basis for the melody treatment that follows:

Note that this 32-measure melody is divided into four eight-measure sections that are substantially different from one another, hence the "A B C D" form as indicated on the chart.

The following melody treatment goes through this 32-measure form twice in total. In the first A, B, C, and D sections (measures 1–32), we apply a straightforward "seven-three below melody" treatment, with no rhythmic rephrasing of the melody or supporting voicings, in a style similar to Track 49. Then in the second A, B, C, and D sections (measures 33–63), we rhythmically rephrase both the melody and the supporting voicings, in a style similar to Track 51.

Ensure that the melody part, played by the upper fingers of the right hand, projects over the seven-three voicings below. For the rhythmic treatment in measures 33–63, try to play the melody as *legato* (smooth and connected) as you can. This creates a good contrast with the swing rhythmic phrases in the supporting voicings. When you're ready, experiment with your own rhythmic treatment of this melody while playing along to the audio track!

4. Kitten Up a Tree

Next up is a tune is written in the style of "Misty," another enduringly popular jazz standard. This classic ballad was written by Erroll Garner, using an "A A B A" form. In this example, we combine comping and melody treatments in the piano part. The piano comps below the guitar melody in the first two A sections, then takes over the melody on the B section and the last A section of the form. This "A A B A" form is shown in the lead sheet below. However, in the arrangement that follows, we have added a further B section and A section, allowing the piano to revert back to a comping role below the guitar melody.

Here is the lead sheet, showing the melody and chord symbols, the basis for the comping and melody treatment that follows:

In the following arrangement, during the first A section (measures 1–8), the piano is comping with four-part block shapes in the right hand, over a mix of root, root-7th, and root-5th voicings in the left hand. These half-note and whole-note voicings are used to support the guitar melody. In the second A section (measures 9–16), the right hand switches to a quarter-note pattern, with the left hand playing the roots and 5ths of the chords, with some eighth-note "pickups" leading into beat 3. Then in the first B section (measures 17–24), the right hand plays the melody as single notes, supported by left-hand block voicings around the middle C area (in the style of Track 56). The right-hand melody continues into the next A section (measures 25–32), now with the left hand playing the supporting block voicings as quarter notes.

As mentioned earlier, an extra B section (measures 33–40) is then added after the basic "A A B A" form shown in the lead sheet, with the piano reverting to a comping role behind the guitar melody. Here the quarter-note block voicings in the right hand are similar to the piano part in the second A section (measures 9–16). Then a final A section (measures 41–48) is added at the end, with the piano part now "splitting" the right-hand block shapes during beat 2, and the left hand playing some octave and root-7th patterns, landing on the "& of 1" and creating a rhythmic pickup into the right-hand voicings on beat 2. All this helps create more momentum and intensity during this final section of the tune.

Make sure your quarter-note block voicings are steady and consistent. This is a useful jazz ballad comping device—borrowed from jazz guitarists! Also make sure the right-hand melody projects over the supporting voicings in measures 17–32.

TRACK 72
full speed

5. Cool Blues

Our last example uses a 12-bar blues form in the style of "Freddie Freeloader" and various other jazz-blues classics. Review the text following Track 34 as needed, regarding the elements of the 12-bar blues form.

This example contains four repeats of the 12-bar blues form in total. The piano part is comping on the first two repeats, then soloing over the last two repeats. In the first repeat of the blues form (measures 1–12), the right hand is playing whole-note block voicings over root-7th intervals in the left hand. In the second repeat (measures 13–24), these same voicings are now played with jazz swing rhythms and anticipations, also using some "held" root notes played by the pinky of the left hand, in the style of Track 48.

Then in the third repeat (measures 25–36), the right hand is playing a solo using the F blues scale, built from the tonic of the key (as we are in F). This is supported in the left hand by various seven-three extended voicings, played as whole notes. In the fourth repeat (measures 37–49) the solo continues, now using the D blues scale built from the relative minor of the key. (D is the relative minor of F. Review text before Track 64 as needed.) The left-hand seven-three extended voicings are now played with typical jazz swing rhythmic phrasing and anticipations, often in a rhythmic "conversation" or alternation with the right-hand solo.

This track is definitely a great springboard for your own comping and improvisation ideas, once you are comfortable with the basics. Get the F and D blues scales under your fingers, then have fun soloing over these classic blues changes!

A1

KEYBOARD STYLE SERIES

THE COMPLETE GUIDE!

These book/audio packs provide focused lessons that contain valuable how-to insight, essential playing tips, and beneficial information for all players. From comping to soloing, comprehensive treatment is given to each subject. The companion audio features many of the examples in the book performed either solo or with a full band.

BEBOP JAZZ PIANO
by John Valerio
This book provides detailed information for bebop and jazz keyboardists on: chords and voicings, harmony and chord progressions, scales and tonality, common melodic figures and patterns, comping, characteristic tunes, the styles of Bud Powell and Thelonious Monk, and more.
00290535 Book/Online Audio $18.99

BEGINNING ROCK KEYBOARD
by Mark Harrison
This comprehensive book/audio package will teach you the basic skills needed to play beginning rock keyboard. From comping to soloing, you'll learn the theory, the tools, and the techniques used by the pros. The accompanying audio demonstrates most of the music examples in the book.
00311922 Book/Online Audio $14.99

BLUES PIANO
by Mark Harrison
With this book/audio pack, you'll learn the theory, the tools, and even the tricks that the pros use to play the blues. Covers: scales and chords; left-hand patterns; walking bass; endings and turnarounds; right-hand techniques; how to solo with blues scales; crossover licks; and more.
00311007 Book/Online Audio $19.99

BOOGIE-WOOGIE PIANO
by Todd Lowry
From learning the basic chord progressions to inventing your own melodic riffs, you'll learn the theory, tools and techniques used by the genre's best practitioners.
00117067 Book/Online Audio $17.99

BRAZILIAN PIANO
by Robert Willey and Alfredo Cardim
Brazilian Piano teaches elements of some of the most appealing Brazilian musical styles: choro, samba, and bossa nova. It starts with rhythmic training to develop the fundamental groove of Brazilian music.
00311469 Book/Online Audio $19.99

CONTEMPORARY JAZZ PIANO
by Mark Harrison
From comping to soloing, you'll learn the theory, the tools, and the techniques used by the pros. The full band tracks on the audio feature the rhythm section on the left channel and the piano on the right channel, so that you can play along with the band.
00311848 Book/Online Audio $18.99

COUNTRY PIANO
by Mark Harrison
Learn the theory, the tools, and the tricks used by the pros to get that authentic country sound. This book/audio pack covers: scales and chords, walkup and walkdown patterns, comping in traditional and modern country, Nashville "fretted piano" techniques and more.
00311052 Book/Online Audio $19.99

GOSPEL PIANO
by Kurt Cowling
Discover the tools you need to play in a variety of authentic gospel styles, through a study of rhythmic devices, grooves, melodic and harmonic techniques, and formal design. The accompanying audio features over 90 tracks, including piano examples as well as the full gospel band.
00311327 Book/Online Adio $17.99

INTRO TO JAZZ PIANO
by Mark Harrison
From comping to soloing, you'll learn the theory, the tools, and the techniques used by the pros. The accompanying audio demonstrates most of the music examples in the book. The full band tracks feature the rhythm section on the left channel and the piano on the right channel, so that you can play along with the band.
00312088 Book/Online Audio $17.99

JAZZ-BLUES PIANO
by Mark Harrison
This comprehensive book will teach you the basic skills needed to play jazz-blues piano. Topics covered include: scales and chords • harmony and voicings • progressions and comping • melodies and soloing • characteristic stylings.
00311243 Book/Online Audio $17.99

JAZZ-ROCK KEYBOARD
by T. Lavitz
Learn what goes into mixing the power and drive of rock music with the artistic elements of jazz improvisation in this comprehensive book and CD package. This instructional tool delves into scales and modes, and how they can be used with various chord progressions to develop the best in soloing chops.
00290536 Book/CD Pack...$17.95

LATIN JAZZ PIANO
by John Valerio
This book is divided into three sections. The first covers Afro-Cuban (Afro-Caribbean) jazz, the second section deals with Brazilian influenced jazz – Bossa Nova and Samba, and the third contains lead sheets of the tunes and instructions for the play-along audio.
00311345 Book/Online Audio $17.99

MODERN POP KEYBOARD
by Mark Harrison
From chordal comping to arpeggios and ostinatos, from grand piano to synth pads, you'll learn the theory, the tools, and the techniques used by the pros. The online audio demonstrates most of the music examples in the book.
00146596 Book/Online Audio $17.99

NEW AGE PIANO
by Todd Lowry
From melodic development to chord progressions to left-hand accompaniment patterns, you'll learn the theory, the tools and the techniques used by the pros. The accompanying 96-track CD demonstrates most of the music examples in the book.
00117322 Book/CD Pack...$16.99

POST-BOP JAZZ PIANO
by John Valerio
This book/audio pack will teach you the basic skills needed to play post-bop jazz piano. Learn the theory, the tools, and the tricks used by the pros to play in the style of Bill Evans, Thelonious Monk, Herbie Hancock, McCoy Tyner, Chick Corea and others. Topics covered include: chord voicings, scales and tonality, modality, and more.
00311005 Book/Online Audio $17.99

PROGRESSIVE ROCK KEYBOARD
by Dan Maske
You'll learn how soloing techniques, form, rhythmic and metrical devices, harmony, and counterpoint all come together to make this style of rock the unique and exciting genre it is.
00311307 Book/Online Audio $19.99

R&B KEYBOARD
by Mark Harrison
From soul to funk to disco to pop, you'll learn the theory, the tools, and the tricks used by the pros with this book/audio pack. Topics covered include: scales and chords, harmony and voicings, progressions and comping, rhythmic concepts, characteristic stylings, the development of R&B, and more! Includes seven songs.
00310881 Book/Online Audio $19.99

ROCK KEYBOARD
by Scott Miller
Learn to comp or solo in any of your favorite rock styles. Listen to the audio to hear your parts fit in with the total groove of the band. Includes 99 tracks! Covers: classic rock, pop/rock, blues rock, Southern rock, hard rock, progressive rock, alternative rock and heavy metal.
00310823 Book/Online Audio $17.99

ROCK 'N' ROLL PIANO
by Andy Vinter
Take your place alongside Fats Domino, Jerry Lee Lewis, Little Richard, and other legendary players of the '50s and '60s! This book/audio pack covers: left-hand patterns; basic rock 'n' roll progressions; right-hand techniques; straight eighths vs. swing eighths; glisses; crushed notes, rolls, note clusters and more. Includes six complete tunes.
00310912 Book/Online Audio $18.99

SALSA PIANO
by Hector Martignon
From traditional Cuban music to the more modern Puerto Rican and New York styles, you'll learn the all-important rhythmic patterns of salsa and how to apply them to the piano. The book provides historical, geographical and cultural background info, and the 50+-tracks includes piano examples and a full salsa band percussion section.
00311049 Book/Online Audio $19.99

SMOOTH JAZZ PIANO
by Mark Harrison
Learn the skills you need to play smooth jazz piano – the theory, the tools, and the tricks used by the pros. Topics covered include: scales and chords; harmony and voicings; progressions and comping; rhythmic concepts; melodies and soloing; characteristic stylings; discussions on jazz evolution.
00311095 Book/Online Audio $19.99

STRIDE & SWING PIANO
by John Valerio
Learn the styles of the stride and swing piano masters, such as Scott Joplin, Jimmy Yancey, Pete Johnson, Jelly Roll Morton, James P. Johnson, Fats Waller, Teddy Wilson, and Art Tatum. This book/audio pack covers classic ragtime, early blues and boogie woogie, New Orleans jazz and more. Includes 14 songs.
00310882 Book/Online Audio $19.99

WORSHIP PIANO
by Bob Kauflin
From chord inversions to color tones, from rhythmic patterns to the Nashville Numbering System, you'll learn the tools and techniques needed to play piano or keyboard in a modern worship setting.
00311425 Book/Online Audio $17.99

HAL•LEONARD®

Prices, contents, and availability
subject to change without notice.

www.halleonard.com

jazz piano solos series

Each volume features exciting new arrangements with chord symbols of the songs which helped define a style.

vol. 1 miles davis
00306521..............$19.99

vol. 2 jazz blues
00306522..............$17.99

vol. 3 latin jazz
00310621..............$16.99

vol. 4 bebop jazz
00310709..............$16.99

vol. 5 cool jazz
00310710..............$16.99

vol. 6 hard bop
00323507..............$16.99

vol. 7 smooth jazz
00310727..............$16.99

vol. 8 jazz pop
00311786..............$17.99

vol. 9 duke ellington
00311787..............$17.99

vol. 10 jazz ballads
00311788..............$17.99

vol. 11 soul jazz
00311789..............$17.99

vol. 12 swinging jazz
00311797..............$17.99

vol. 13 jazz gems
00311899..............$16.99

vol. 14 jazz classics
00311900..............$16.99

vol. 15 bossa nova
00311906..............$17.99

vol. 16 disney
00312121..............$17.99

vol. 17 antonio carlos jobim
00312122..............$17.99

vol. 18 modern jazz quartet
00307270..............$16.99

vol. 19 bill evans
00307273..............$19.99

vol. 20 gypsy jazz
00307289..............$16.99

vol. 21 new orleans
00312169..............$16.99

vol. 22 classic jazz
00001529..............$17.99

vol. 23 jazz for lovers
00312548..............$16.99

vol. 24 john coltrane
00307395..............$17.99

vol. 25 christmas songs
00101790..............$17.99

vol. 26 george gershwin
00103353..............$17.99

vol. 27 late night jazz
00312547..............$17.99

vol. 28 the beatles
00119302..............$19.99

vol. 29 elton john
00120968..............$19.99

vol. 30 cole porter
00123364..............$17.99

vol. 31 cocktail piano
00123366..............$17.99

vol. 32 johnny mercer
00123367..............$16.99

vol. 33 gospel
00127079..............$17.99

vol. 34 horace silver
00139633..............$16.99

vol. 35 stride piano
00139685..............$17.99

vol. 36 broadway jazz
00144365..............$17.99

vol. 37 silver screen jazz
00144366..............$16.99

vol. 38 henry mancini
00146382..............$16.99

vol. 39 sacred christmas carols
00147678..............$17.99

vol. 40 charlie parker
00149089..............$16.99

vol. 41 pop standards
00153656..............$16.99

vol. 42 dave brubeck
00154634..............$16.99

vol. 43 candlelight jazz
00154901..............$17.99

vol. 44 jazz standards
00160856..............$17.99

vol. 45 christmas standards
00172024..............$17.99

vol. 46 cocktail jazz
00172025..............$17.99

vol. 47 hymns
00172026..............$17.99

vol. 48 blue skies & other irving berlin songs
00197873..............$16.99

vol. 49 thelonious monk
00232767..............$16.99

vol. 50 best smooth jazz
00233277..............$16.99

vol. 51 disney favorites
00233315..............$16.99

vol. 52 bebop classics
00234075..............$16.99

vol. 53 jazz-rock
00256715..............$16.99

vol. 54 jazz fusion
00256716..............$16.99

vol. 55 ragtime
00274961..............$16.99

vol. 56 pop ballads
00274962..............$16.99

vol. 57 pat metheny
00277058..............$17.99

vol. 58 big band era
00284837..............$17.99

vol. 59 west coast jazz
00290792..............$17.99

vol. 60 boogie woogie
00363280..............$17.99

vol. 61 christmas classics
00367872..............$17.99

HAL•LEONARD®
View songlists and order online from your favorite music retailer at
www.halleonard.com

0621
Prices, contents & availability subject to change without notice.